FOR
THOSE
WHO
CAN'T
BELIEVE

FOR THOSE WHO CAN'T BELIEVE

Overcoming the Obstacles to Faith

HAROLD M. SCHULWEIS

HarperPerennial

A Division of HarperCollinsPublishers

First HarperPerennial edition published 1995.

Designed by Nancy Singer

The Library of Congress has catalogued the hardcover edition as follows:

Schulweis, Harold M.
    For those who can't believe : overcoming the obstacles to faith / Harold M. Schulweis.
       p.   cm.
    Includes index.
    ISBN 0-06-018241-5
    1. Judaism—Essence, genius, nature. 2. Belief and doubt. 3. Faith and reason—Judaism. 4. God (Judaism)—Knowableness. 5. Prayer—Judaism. I. Title.
    BM565.S363   1994
    296.3—dc20   93-48657

ISBN 0-06-092651-1 (pbk.)

98 99 ❖/RRD 10 9 8 7 6

To the men, women, and children of Valley Beth Shalom
who possess the wisdom to question and the courage to hear.

Contents

Contents

To Whom This Book
Is Addressed

"For the believer there are no questions and for the unbeliever there are no answers," said Menachem Mendel, a rabbi of the nineteenth century. That conclusion does not accord with my own experiences. I have come to know many believers with profound doubts and many unbelievers with deep yearnings for serious answers.

In matters of religion, most people do not ask questions or seek answers. They assume a neither/nor neutrality: neither apostate nor believer; neither denier nor affirmer of their faith. They pay their dues, attend an occasional service, answer yes when pollsters ask them whether they believe in God, and register their children in "Hebrew school." They send their children to know about religion, not to believe; to know about ritual, not to observe; to know how to pray, not to pray; to know something about Jewish history, not to be engaged in the people's way of life. But knowing is not believing; knowing is not behaving; knowing is not belonging.

Publicly, most are as respectful of religion as the skeptic philosopher Voltaire who doffed his hat when passing a religious processional. Asked whether his gesture signified his return to the faith, Voltaire demurred: "When God and I pass each other, we salute. We do not speak." The major constituency of those affiliated, nonaffiliated, and underaffiliated do not speak to God or of God. The muteness is testimony to their coolness toward religious faith and practice.

Why are so many of us indifferent to religion, even those who in our youth expressed enthusiasm and healthy curiosity toward matters of faith? What happened to our wonder about the truth of the miracles in the Bible, or our concern over the fairness in the treatment of young Isaac bound to the altar, or our doubts as to the effectiveness of prayer? And what was wrong with the answers we received?

Our questions were either given short shrift, answered with dogmatic curtness, or put off to an unspecified future time: "When you're older you'll understand." The religious questions were displaced by Hebrew reading exercises, a few ritual skills, some Bible stories, and preparations for the bar/bat mitzvah public performance. The unanswered questions dried up, and in their place a theological black hole formed. This vacuum was in turn filled with superstition, myths, literalist translations of profound religious insight, images of street theology that as adults we cannot accept.

Although a token respect for religion is maintained, the discontent with religion is evident in the confessions of widespread ennui. Many are bored with services, bored with prayer, bored with sermons. The boredom is not relieved by larger choirs or shorter sermons or creative prayers. Boredom is a symptom, not a cause, and it is not overcome by external repairs. Neither new translations nor transliterations, neither songs nor poetry, counter the disinterest that hovers over the collapse of faith. Muteness and boredom are symptoms of disbelief in the wisdom, morality, and reality of conventional religion.

The disaffected are not mean spirited. Their complaints should not be dismissed as the petulance of the ignorant or heretical. Many of the complaints are justifiable, and many of the questions are honorable. In our adult life, the dormant questions of our youth need to be revisited and the conventional answers we were given need to be reappraised. The prematurely buried questions of our youth need to be resurrected.

Consider David, representative of the many nonobserving people who my colleagues and I meet often. Secularly educated, David is not alone in his attitude toward aspects of Judaism, which ranges from ambivalence to antipathy. On occasion he breaks through the etiquette of neutrality and confesses, "I'm not the religious type, but I am a spiritual person." What does David have in mind when he says that he is not the "religious type" but a "spiritual" person?

David associates religion with his preparation for the bar mitzvah. He mechanically learned the words, melodies, and skills, and memorized the prophetical portion to be chanted from a tape. But he recalls that he had no notion of what the prophetic words meant, or for that matter who or what a prophet is. He recalls his early religious education as mostly wasteful, rote, and irrelevant. He vaguely remembers stories about serpents in the Garden of Eden, magic rods that break the sea, donkeys who speak back to their master, a ménage of animals crowded in an ark. The "religious type" he conjures up is an obedient, conforming follower of ritual laws and commands, a dull "amen sayer" devoid of any heroic virtues.

Who can fault his apathy? Many Davids have been taught the Bible as a bare-bones literal text without the philosophy, spirituality, and morality that give meaning to the tradition. They have been taught the prayer book without anticipating the questions about the efficacy of prayer and its pertinence to living. They have been taught the uniqueness of Judaism without mention of the grandeur of the tradition of dissent and intellectual integrity. They have been taught ritual without the moral poetry of its practice.

Judaism has become small in David's eyes. He is included among the 1.2 million born Jews who, when asked, "What is your religion?" answer "None." It is a response not restricted to Jews or to the unaffiliated. It is a response of a growing portion of contemporary society. When David and Jane, his non-Jewish fiancée, come to the rabbi, they arrive as "none" Jews and "none" Christians. They request an interfaith marriage that in effect amounts to an interfaithless union. On the one hand, David and Jane feel that a justice of the peace is not enough; on the other, they feel that religious belief is not deeply significant. They are neither fundamentalists nor liberals, believers nor atheists. They are readers of "the blank page between the Old and the New Testaments," as Benjamin Disraeli sadly admitted of himself when asked by Queen Victoria, "Which Bible do you read, my lord?"

Even though David is not the "religious type," he has never denied that he is a Jew. He calls himself a cultural or an ethnic Jew. How long will that identity last separated from a living religious culture? For David has no language, no song, no poetry, no drama, no Zion, no God.

Still, David is sincere in declaring that he is a "spiritual person." It expresses his gnawing ambivalence. Turned off by the old-time religion he remembers from his youth, he is unsatisfied by the materialistic world and its mindless ambition to "pursue pleasure and avoid pain." He wants more for himself and his family. He is caught between mourning the deceased and yearning for the not yet born. The dead gods leave ghosts in their wake, half mocked, half revered.

There are spiritual hungers in David. It is for him and his fiancée, Jane, that this book is written. Their numbers are legion. They are among the affiliated and the unaffiliated. They are Jews and non-Jews. This book is addressed to those who cannot go home again but do not wish to live spiritually homeless. Home is too important to be abandoned. It must be madè habitable again.

I acknowledge that conventional religion bears a large measure of responsibility for the state of unbelief and the trivialization of profound religious questions. Far too much of religious education turns significant events into acts of magic, the majesty of prayer into mechanical mumbling, the suffering of victims into the pain of the guilt-ridden, the loyalty to a people into provincial self-interest.

In this book I address a number of the unanswered quests. I am convinced that the religious questions asked in our youth express some of the most important questions of our life. Those questions need to be revived and answered honestly. Gazing at the motionless child who appeared to be dead, the prophet Elijah "went up and lay upon the child, put his mouth upon his mouth, his eyes upon his eyes, his hands upon his hands, and stretched himself upon the child. And the flesh of the child waxed warm and the child opened his eyes and sneezed" (II Kings 4:34).

Although I include some typical questions asked by young people, this is not an answer book to children's questions. The questions are ours. The questions we ask today are often "grown-up" versions of the questions we asked as children. We no longer wonder why we never received the pony we asked God for. But we question the meaning of prayer and despair that many of our prayers go unanswered.

What does the child ask? What lies behind the questions about talking serpents and whales that swallow prophets alive? Behind the questions is the search to discover what religion declares to be real about the universe, about humanity, about life, about the self. We would know from religion what is real, and, more important, what is "really real" or of true significance: What is solid in the world; upon what can we stand and upon whom can we depend?

Chapter 1 examines the meaning of the persistent question, "Where is God?" Where within the domain of reality is God located? In answering this basic question I propose a religious exercise, "touch my love," that illlustrates the character of reality that religion intends.

Two religious texts are found in the lecterns of the house of worship and in the desks of the religious school: the Bible and the prayer book. Chapter 2 begins with prayer because it is the earliest and most pervasive form of religious expression. Prayer, particularly petitionary prayer, raises a series of questions that touch upon the nature of God and the relationship of God to the worshiper. Questions about prayer are questions about reality. Does God "really" hear prayer? Does God "really" answer prayer? If God hears and answers, can I pray for anything? If God does not answer my prayers, is there some flaw in my character, or some inadequacy in God? If God knows the secrets of the heart, are my prayers superfluous? In the prayers that call for praise to God, am I reduced to the role of a sycophant or a solicitor? Why does God call for our adulation? The answers to these questions call for a rethinking of conventional explanations. We turn to those elements of the tradition that have typically been ignored or repressed, to the tradition, largely untaught and unassimilated, that is wary of the "vain prayers" that ignore the facts of reality. The depth of tradition struggles against the ignorant piety that ties prayer to magic. Prayer is not wishful thinking, nor properly taught is it an offense to reason and morality.

If authentic prayer must be distinguished from magic,

how do we distinguish magic from the miracles found in the Bible? Chapter 3 discusses the proper appreciation of the miraculous in accordance with the deepest insights of the rabbinic and philosophical tradition. How does a religious sensibility, living in a scientific age, explain the miracles recorded in the Bible and celebrated in many of the Jewish holidays? Does belief in miracles preclude common sense and scientific belief? Are miracles obsolete, or can we find them in our contemporary lives?

The response to these questions leads us in Chapter 4 to view miracles as signs of transcendence. How is transcendence communicated to mortal beings? What does it mean to believe in divine revelation? The most frustrating questions raised about the Bible are traced to the plodding literalism with which teachers read the Bible. Literalism renders the most profound biblical text vulnerable to ridicule. Without mature interpretation, the moral and spiritual significance of the biblical narration is lost. Without interpretation, the moral flaws of biblical heroes, the imperfections of patriarchs, matriarchs, prophets, and priests, leave the reader with embarrassment and bafflement. Without interpretation, in what sense is the Bible sacred?

Literalism not only challenges the rational character of the tradition but as often violates the moral sensitivity of the religious seeker. In Chapter 5 I confront some of the deepest challenges to faith. Is obedience to authority the hallmark of faith? Is a revealed commandment to be followed even if it runs against our moral conscience? How may we distinguish the voice of Satan from the voice of God? What is the role of conscience in the tradition of faith?

One question more than any other shakes the foundation of faith. Asked in different voices and at different stages of one's life, the question of evil persists. It erupts in times of sickness or death, in experiences of unaccountable suffering that mock the trust placed in God as Creator, Sustainer, and Guarantor of a just universe. An entire theological discipline is dedicated to accommodate the disparity between God's all-powerful goodness and the triumph of evil over good people. The discipline is called *theodicy*, the defense of God's goodness and omnipotence in view of the existence of evil. "Why me?" or "Why us?" is not a request for factual information. It is an outcry that must be answered. While the practical response to such pain calls for the consolation of friends and family, and while theological explanations seem out of place when the dead lie before the bereaved, the theological question embedded in "Why me?" should not be circumvented. Long after the loss is mourned, the plaintive cry of the suffering demands of faith a plausible explanation of the dissonance between the reality of evil and the morality of God.

Embedded in every question are assumptions so taken for granted that they are not evident even to the questioner. "Why me?" entails an underlying world view about the control and purpose of life. That world view determines the kind of answer the questioner hears. The conventional answers have for most people failed. If we are to find alternative answers that satisfy the mind and moral sense of the sufferer, the assumptions lying dormant in the question must be carefully unfolded and themselves questioned. Chapter 6 attempts to do this.

Suffering and evil are particularly challenging to the faith in a single God. In monotheism, there is no other power to blame for evil. If there is no devil, no original sin, how does the oneness and wholeness of God square with the presence of radical evil? Chapter 7 proposes to resolve the internal conflict by calling for a deeper examination of the allegiance to the single deity. What is the nature of this one God? Two dimensions of Divinity, both rooted in the biblical and rabbinic Jewish tradition, are explored. Elohim, the morally neutral Source of nature, and Adonai, the Source of morality, represent the two faces of one God. Each explains different events in human life, and cultivates in us different but coherent responses. Acceptance is the appropriate religious response to events that are related to the Source of nature, Elohim. Transformation is the proper religious response to those events that are related to the Source of morality, Adonai. Acceptance is not capitulation, nor is transformation an exercise of a capricious will. Acceptance and transformation express faith in the oneness and wholeness of Divinity. Both faces of God are complementary and are reflected in the struggles for the integration of the human person.

The dual dimension of God has its corollary in the understanding of human nature. What the tradition has identified as two basic human inclinations, the good and evil impulses, reflect those features described in Elohim and Adonai. They are not warring enemies but interdependent energies which, when balanced, express the wholeness of one God.

Looking back at the obstacles to belief, I argue in Chapter 8 for another approach to understanding the idea of God and its relationship to prayer, miracle, and revelation. I introduce the idea of Godliness (in Hebrew, Elohuth), which offers a perspective that is not bogged down with conventional religion's tendency to split the human and the divine. Healing that schism entails a shift from God the noun to God the verb, from God to Godliness. Faith in

Godliness brings to the fore the theistic humanism in Judaism and, in effect, horizontalizes the vertical view of the relationship between God and humanity.

Children know about evil. They have their losses, their fears of rejection and abandonment. Children are party to a larger history as well. They are taught or overhear in conversation the tragedies that befell the Jewish people and other peoples, from Bergen Belsen to Bosnia. Where is Godliness in these cruelties? How can we understand the Holocaust without denying the harshness of its truth and yet not destroy basic trust in the possibility of goodness in humankind? The dissonance between faith in God who creates the human being in His image and the undeniable history of the Holocaust challenges the core of faith. To retrieve hope in the possibility of human life, Chapter 9 offers evidence of the goodness of men, women, and children. Ordinary people risked their lives to protect the lives of others not of their faith. Largely unknown and untaught, the rescue by Christians of Jews during the Nazi years is of particular relevance in restoring morale and trust to the traumatized generations after Auschwitz and Herzegovina.

Religion is not philosophy alone, and the stumbling blocks to faith are not only cognitive obstacles to belief. There are "Why be Jewish?" challenges that question the need to belong and to behave. Responses to this order of questions lead us to the personal rites of passage from birth to death. These are the sacred occasions that create memories that in turn create nostalgic ties that bind the self to family and to community. Properly interpreted, the rites of passage transmit the ethos and mythos of tradition that establish the cords of identity and continuity. Where the rites are not observed or are performed without the underlying symbolic meaning, a vacuum is created that is not readily filled by talk about history or ideas. The experiences of rites of passage strengthen the relationships of the self and others. Importantly, the rites of passage we analyze in Chapter 10 trace the journey of the self toward Godliness.

Chapter 11 addresses one of the major obstacles to a commitment to a faith, its perceived parochialism. The would-be believer experiences the strain of forced options: either Jew or human being. Is our essential loyalty to our people or to humanity? If it is to our people alone, do we not betray humanity? If our fealty is to humanity, are we not led to abandon our community? Does commitment to a particular faith enlarge the self or stunt its growth? If the issue is framed in intractable oppositions, the contradiction is beyond resolution. But Judaism always has had at its core a particularistic universalism cultivating the balance between community and humanity. "If we are not for ourselves, who will be for us? But if we are only for ourselves, what are we?"

I have found in conversations with the young and adult Davids that most of the religious problems are framed in either/or boxes that grow into stumbling blocks. Either/or questions promote either/or answers. Things are true or false, literal or fanciful, revealed or invented, divine or human, particular or universal. This dichotomous form of thinking sets a trap for the answerer. For the structure of either/or thinking implies that the options presented exhaust all other alternatives. Either a fool or a knave. But perhaps neither, or both. Either he believes that there are proofs for God's existence or he is an atheist. But perhaps neither/nor. More than logic is involved here. Either/or thinking is intolerant of religious pluralism, impatient with both/and resolutions and with anything more than all or nothing answers. It accepts only absolute answers as the mark of faith and dismisses theological modesty as a sign of disbelief. Like the historian of ideas, Isaiah Berlin, "I do not believe that all genuine questions have only one true answer; that those answers are noble, and that the answers all compatible with one another together form a single coherent goal."

The aim of this book is to present alternative responses to rigid approaches that shut off the possibilities of spiritual renewal for seekers of all faiths. The approach is rooted in the Jewish tradition. But that tradition is too complex, in parts too contradictory, to offer a seamless presentation of the authentic tradition. Any attempt to carve a simple philosophy out of the multiple elements of a 4,000-year-old civilization inevitably selects certain texts, insights, and authorities and assigns them greater weight than others. The magnanimous reader will call these choices philosophy; the less generous will judge them biases. They may both be right. But I am emboldened to present my own approach to the religious tradition by the response of the courageous nineteenth-century rabbi, Menachem Mendel of Kotzk, who was chastised by some elder for deviating from the conventional ritual practices and thinking. When asked, "Why can't you follow in the footsteps of your revered father?" he replied, "I do. My father didn't follow in the footsteps of his father."

In some of the chapters I have referred to children's letters to God, questions and observations of young and older people. In their bluntness they reveal our own unarticulated doubts. One such letter relates to my own discomfort with gender language in these essays. Sarah writes, "Dear God, are boys better than girls? I know You are one, but try to be fair." Sarah picked up her theological information somewhere, from someone. It should come as no surprise, since God's masculine gender is so embedded in the syntax of our religious grammar. I have tried to avoid any insinuation of God's masculine nature. But I found that the attempt to neutralize God's gender was clumsy and distracting. I want Sarah to know that my conception of God is not only beyond gender but beyond anthropomorphism. "God is not a man" (Numbers 23:19).

Touching God

*It may sound strange but I began
to ponder creation
when I was still a little boy. . . .
What is time? What is space?
What is eternity? Infinity?
How can something be created
from nothing?
God has created the world
but who created God?*

Isaac Bashevis Singer

Children are born philosophers. They possess the sense of wonder, and out of wonder faith springs.

Questions are the birth pangs of philosophy and theology. We must pay attention to first questions and to first answers, for they carry crucial consequences for spiritual growth. First questions and answers are the building blocks out of which basic attitudes toward religion are formed. They will not be the last questions asked, unless the answers close off all further inquiry.

"Really" Questions

What do children ask? They begin with "really" questions. Did the serpent "really" speak to Eve in the Garden of Eden? Did Noah "really" gather all the beasts and the animals and the fowl in his ark? Are our prayers "really" heard and "really" answered? Was it "really" right for God to harden Pharaoh's heart and kill the firstborn?

A bit older they may add speculative "if" questions. If God is all powerful, can He make a stone so heavy that He Himself cannot lift it? If He can, He is not all powerful. If He can't, He is not all powerful. If God knows His own future, must He not do what He knows He will do? If not, God is limited in knowledge.

Like many young people, Isaac Bashevis Singer began to study the Book of Genesis with both faith and doubt, and also like so many, he found that the more he read, the more questions assailed him. "If God could have created Adam by the words of His mouth, why did He have to cast a deep sleep upon Adam to form Eve from one of his ribs? . . . Why since God is a God of mercy did He accept the sacrifice of Abel and not of Cain? Didn't He foresee that this would cause jealousy and enmity between the two brothers?"

On the surface, the questions are about God and prayer and Bible stories. But they are not only about serpents and magical rods and logical contradictions. They are about the religious understanding of reality. What is the world really like? What can I trust? Whom can I trust? What can I expect? What can I hope for? What in me is real? What in the world is really real, truly important for my life?

The religious inquiries of our youth are the most important questions we may ever ask. The answers that define reality affect our self-understanding, our morality and morale. The poet Wallace Stevens wrote, "We live in the description of a place, not in the place itself." Religion is the description of the place we inhabit.

"Later"

Why is it that when we grow up, we no longer ask these questions? What happens to the wonder of childhood?

My first teacher of religion was my grandfather. An erudite man, he taught me how to translate the biblical text and how to pray. He was patient and proud of my questions. Perhaps not all my questions. He was patient with my questions about the meaning of words, grammar, places, dates, facts—questions of "where" or "what" or "how." But my "what for" questions, particularly those that asked for the meaning and purpose of the texts, disturbed him.

"Was it fair for Abraham to frighten Isaac at the altar?"

"Why did David and Bath-Sheba's infant die because of their sins?" These follow-up questions to his factual accounts of the Bible lessons my grandfather regarded as interruptions of the serious study of the text. My grandfather would affectionately pinch my cheek and respond "shpayter," the Yiddish word for "later."

"Later" meant that when I was older I would understand; when I was older I would be answered. But "later" never came. I grew older, the teachers changed, the texts were different, the questions sharper, but the response was much the same. "Later," I began to suspect, was a conspiracy of avoidance. Adults are practiced in strategies of delay.

The rationale for theological procrastination varies. Sometimes the questions are not dealt with because we think they are beyond the conceptual or linguistic grasp of the very young. Children are too literal minded to think abstractly.

With respect to older children, it is argued that text, ritual, and prayer skills are more important than abstract theological discussions. Judaism is a religion of deeds, not creeds, some say, a matter of behaving, not believing. And so with one blow against dogma, the entire enterprise of Jewish theological culture is dismissed; religious questions are put on hold. Sometimes, it is maintained, troubling questions such as those about the apparent disparity between suffering of innocents and the goodness of God belong to the eternal questions of human existence. The antique origin and irresolubility of those questions are further reasons to relegate the answers to some vaguely future time. If all the patriarchs and philosophers couldn't find satisfactory answers to these questions, who are we to ask for or expect answers? Respect for antiquity has intimidated many a probing questioner.

Street Theology

What happens to questions ignored? Like hope deferred, questions unanswered make the heart sick. In their wake, cavities of disbelief are formed. In religious schools, prayer, Bible, miracles, belief, and practice are taught in a theological vacuum. But how can the prayer book be taught intelligently without anticipating questions about the limits of petition or the legitimacy of asking God for intervention? How can the Bible be taught without foreseeing the snares of literalism that run against the grain of common sense and scientific plausibility?

The "later" syndrome creates its own void. Like sexual knowledge, when our religious questions are avoided, we learn the answers in the street. When religious instruction is unmindful of the moment and occasion that prompt the question, street theology soon fills the void with superstition and fantasy.

Notions of God, prayer, and miracles are woven out of fragments of images reinforced by cartoons, movies, television, and hearsay. Researchers of religious development have observed that most of us begin to construct belief and disbelief systems about God and the universe between ages four and six. Even children who come from nonreligious or antireligious homes possess vivid ideas about God. These ideas are plucked from the air. As Erik Erikson noted, "We never meet any person, not even a newborn, who never has an environment."

Letters to God, compiled by Eric Marshall and Stuart Hample, contains theological gems. "Dear God. I wrote you before. Do you remember? I did what I promised but you didn't send me a horse yet. What about it? Louis."

"Dear God. I got left back. Thanks. Raymond." The letters entail serious religious questions to be answered seriously. Louis and Raymond are questioning the efficacy of prayer. How and what they are answered will affect their faith (or lack of faith) for the rest of their lives. The questions are not "kid stuff" to be staved off. "Later"—if it ever arrives—comes too late. The grown child has been imprinted with the rumors of "old-time religion." Worse, when youngsters are deprived of more mature ways to understand religion, the different approaches presented "later" are often resisted as inauthentic. The time for answering questions is when they are asked.

There are ways of not answering, and even ways of answering that silence the questioner. One foolproof closure is the use of the word *God* to dissolve all questions: "Why are babies born?" "Why is the sky blue?" "Why did Grandma die?" The single answer to all questions is "God." The *God* word grants instant omniscience. This monosyllable frees us from the need to construct complex explanations. "What is small and gray and runs around the park collecting nuts for the winter?" the Sunday school teacher asked. A bright student answered, "I know the answer must be God but it sure sounds like a squirrel." The child has caught on to the theological game. To use "God" as the shortcut to complex questions is to use God's name in vain. It is to seal off religious curiosity.

"Where" Questions

It happens to me at every religious school assembly. The teachers have encouraged the children to ask whatever religious questions are on their minds. The children are excited. Their hands wave wildly; their faces are intense. The question is almost always the same: "Where is God?" I could point skyward. The children have heard prayers that refer to "Our God in heaven" and have seen movies in which the camera moves toward the billowy clouds, suggesting a place above from which the voice of God descends. But it is misleading. Does God dwell in the heavens? Do I mean to perpetuate a spatial image of the divine? In one of the "Dear God" letters written by a child leaving St. Patrick's Cathedral, he observes, "Dear God, you sure live in a nice place."

I could tell them that God is nowhere in particular but that, like the air, God is everywhere. A colleague offered that kind of answer only to hear a youngster blurt out, "I don't want God to be everywhere. I want God to be somewhere." By "somewhere" the child meant that she wanted God to be real. For her, seeing is believing and pointing is proving, and space is the place for the real. "Where" implies place, some physical location for God.

"Where is God?" is one of the first questions asked, but it belongs to a whole set of "where" questions that cling to the imagination of the religious seeker: Where is heaven? Where is hell? Where do angels live? Where did Grandpa go when he died? Our answer to "Where is God?" is not simply a response to a specific question; it provides a way of thinking about spiritual matters. We need to present the view of God, and, by extension, the larger realm of the divine without reducing its reality to the laws of material, physical bodies. What is called for is a comprehensible, experiential encounter that will invite the religious imagination to entertain an honest spiritual universe.

Touch My Love

In our home, the children were put to bed at night with some conversation and a prayer. One evening my daughter, then six or seven, asked the perennial question, "Where is God?" following the prayer proclaiming God, the Lord as One. In her book *Today's Children and Yesterday's Heritage*, Sophia Fahs, a thoughtful religious educator, suggested a game to answer the "where" question. I decided to adapt her game with my daughter. I asked her to touch my arms. She did. I asked her to touch my chest. She did. I asked her to touch my nose. She did. I then asked her to touch my love. She stopped for a moment and reached out to touch my chest and my arms. I pointed out that she had already done so. "Now touch my love." She could not. She smiled. The exercise was an introduction to a deeper understanding of faith.

Commentary on a Religious Exercise

What was the religious exercise designed to accomplish? On the face of it, the question "Where is God?" was not answered. The exercise did not refer directly to God. The exercise did not even mention God. But the "where" question anticipated a question about the reality of God. The exercise enabled my daughter to learn that there are "things" in the world that are very real, in fact the most real, things that we really care deeply about, but they cannot be touched, probed, pushed, or located in space. The intent of the game was to prepare the ground for an understanding of the reality of nonmaterial, spiritual matters.

In the course of the spiritual growth, many questions and answers will refer to the nonmaterial qualities ascribed to God, such as mercy, or justice, or peace, or truthfulness. Like touching love, the attributes of God cannot be seen or touched or located in the manner that tables, chairs, and clocks can. "Touch my love" serves as a powerful analogue for the field of relationship. The "where" question was not dismissed as wrong. The "where" question simply does not apply to a nonmaterial reality.

For some, the religious exercise may appear oblique. But such patient introduction to religious belief is important to maintain a respect for religious wisdom. There is too great a temptation to rush to the word *God*. God should come at the conclusion of the argument. The Book of Genesis does not begin with the name of God. God's name comes after "in the beginning." When religious education is directed toward experience and growth, God is not the first but the last word. The exercise opened an ongoing dialogue about the reality of spirituality.

Natural Mysticism: Betweenness

The "touch my love" exercise opens the child to a natural religious mysticism. There is a wonder and surprise in feeling love but failing to touch it, in knowing love but being unable to verbalize it. Theologians consider ineffability, the inability to express certain experiences in words, as a sign of mystical experience. But the mystery experienced in "touch my love" does not come from another world different from the one in which we live and breathe. The mystery experienced is not based on a split universe, material and spiritual, natural and beyond nature. The power, mystery, and significance of transcendence, something beyond the limits of the five senses, are grounded in earthly love. The sense of transcendence introduced through the "touch my love" game is not otherworldly, supernatural, or even simplistically reduced to physical terms. The transcendence of spirituality, as in love, includes a material environment.

Sometime later, when we replayed the game and I asked my daughter "Where is love?" she did not touch me at all but pointed to her chest as if to say love is in her. I asked her to hug herself, to kiss her hand. She laughed. She experienced the flatness of those gestures. She began to understand, faintly at first, that love requires an other. She experienced the first recognition that love is "between" people. It was the first step to understanding that love is relational. Transcendence introduced in the religious game means that there is a spiritual reality greater than myself or herself, but that includes us both.

It will become clearer in later chapters in what sense Godliness, like love, is located not "in me" or "in you" but "between us." Love is not "in" the subject or "in" the object but "between" them. Like the experience of Godliness, love points to a relationship with an "other."

In Judaism, the importance of "betweenness" is expressed in the high value the tradition places on community. Acts of holiness, such as the recitation of the mourner's kaddish and the public reading of the Torah, require a minyan, a quorum of ten representatives of the community. The noblest form of communion with God is through community. This concept of "betweenness" is a major religious insight. I did not speak of the relational love of "betweenness" to my daughter at that point in her young life. But these first steps in the exercise help develop religious sensibilities. The heart and mind need preparation.

There are other lessons in that religious exercise. "Touch my love" teaches that love cannot be manipulated. I cannot make my daughter love me, nor can she make me love her. Tables and chairs can be "made." Love is a relationship that cannot be manufactured or ordered. The biblical imperative does not command that we love our parents, but that they be respected. God cannot force people to love Him. Therein lies part of the uniqueness and mystery of the love of God.

As a parent, I learned something valuable from the exercise. The "touch my love" game itself depends on my loving relationship to my daughter. Parents create relationships and memories of those relationships, which in turn serve as the spiritual material out of which the idea of God is formed.

From Where to When

In Hasidic literature, a child asks, "Where is God?" His teacher answers, "Whenever we let God in." I tell children that I will answer "where God is" if they will tell me "when God is." Without a moment's hesitation they volunteer a whole series of answers. "God is when I was sick in the hospital and my friends wrote me letters and sent me gifts." "God is when the family is together for my birthday." The shifting from where to when redirects the mind's eye from place to time, from location to occasion.

A moving instance of such a reorientation is reported

by Martin Buber, who relates a conversation between a nineteenth-century rabbi of northern White Russia and the chief of the gendarmes. The latter, learning that the prisoner was a rabbi, asked him, "How is it that according to the Bible, God who knows everything did not know where Adam was hiding in the Garden of Eden?" "Do you believe," the rabbi asked, "that the Scriptures are eternal and that every era, every generation, every man is included in them?" "I believe this," said the jailer. The rabbi continued: "Well, in every era, God calls every man, 'Where are you in your world? So many years and days of those allotted to you have passed and how far have you gotten in your world?' God says something like this: 'You have lived forty-six years. How far along are you?'" When the chief of the gendarmes heard his age mentioned, he pulled himself together, laid his hand on the rabbi's shoulder, and cried "Bravo," but his heart trembled.

The gendarme's surface question was a matter of logic, how to square God's all-knowing nature with His apparent ignorance of the place Adam had hidden. The rabbi's response deliberately did not deal with the literal question of place. He treated the "where" question as if it referred to the inner space of the gendarme's self. The answer turned a logical, external inquiry into an existential, inner concern. The rabbi's answer uncovered for the gendarme a deeper layer to his question: every human being turns his existence into "a system of hideouts," escaping the responsibility for his or her life. The rabbi redirected the gendarme's question and opened his eyes to another meaning of the religious quest.

Conclusions

Questions contain presuppositions. For that reason alone, we must examine questions with care. In the following chapters I inquire into the underlying assumptions embedded in such questions as "Does God hear my prayers?" "Why are miracles not performed today?" "Why did it happen to me?" Unexamined, hidden assumptions frequently force unintended answers on us. To escape that entrapment, answers may properly call for questioning the question itself. All questions must be respected, but not all questions need to be accepted without question.

But questioning questions should not be used to avoid offering answers. As the philosopher Carlye Marney wisely said, "A window shut open is as useless as a window shut closed. In either case you've lost the use of the window." Our failures to foster a healthy faith may be traced to a window shut open that disguises our ignorance as much as to a window shut closed that stifles curiosity. Regarding the former, when we are open to everything in general because we are committed to nothing in particular, we are unlikely to develop a serious religious sensibility. Without religious conviction, we are tempted to evade the question. In G. K. Chesterton's words, "Where man ceases believing in something, it isn't that he believes in nothing; but that he then believes in anything." Religious nature abhors a vacuum.

When we claim not to know how to answer a religious question from another, we may suspect that the question is hidden within. It is told of a Hasidic master that he possessed an uncanny ability to understand the sins of his disciples. When asked how it is that a man of his piety knows the secrets of the heart of sinners, he explained, "I don't find it difficult to understand their transgressions, because whenever I listen attentively, I discover that their transgressions are only different versions of my own. Once I failed to recognize the sins of a man who came to me. Then I knew, from my not knowing, that I must be hiding that transgression in myself."

To Whom We Pray and for What

Prayer is poetry believed in.

George Santayana

Prayer begins early in our lives. It is often the first religious act performed at bedside, at the religious school assembly, in the sanctuary, the house of prayer. Although there are many forms of prayer, including those of praise, thanksgiving, and even of protest, for most of us the heart of prayer derives from something wanted, needed, asked for. Many of the first and lasting religious questions revolve around the efficacy of prayer.

Petitionary Prayer

Does prayer really work? Does the world, as religion understands it, respond to our requests? Does a worshiped God care enough to intervene in our lives? If God does not intervene, is it because God can't or because God won't?

Answers build on each other vertically and horizontally. Vertically, because yesterday's answers are the grounds of tomorrow's questions. Horizontally, because what we learn about one area of religious belief affects our understanding of other areas of religious belief. Thus our understanding of prayer is bound to influence our understanding of miracles, magic, revelation, and the nature of God.

Susie's Prayer

At age six, Susie wanted to know whether God hears prayers. She had picked up the notion that if you are in need or in trouble, and you pray honestly, God will hear and help. She had prayed hard and long for a Cabbage Patch doll like those her friends had. But prayer was of no avail. She wondered whether God really answers prayers. She asked her religious school teacher, who explained that God certainly hears and answers prayers, but, in this case, God simply had said no. The answer seemed reasonable enough. God is not forced to say yes to every petition.

Susie may have been convinced that her prayer was undeserving of God's response, that it was less than noble, even selfish. Susie, for the moment, may have been satisfied with the response that God had said no. But answers have afterlives. Years later, Susie's mother was in the hospital gravely ill. Susie prayed that her mother be made well, yet her mother died. Susie did not pray for ignoble wishes. Surely her prayer was deserving of a response. Did God say no? Was the negative response due to something she had done wrong, or something her mother or her father had done to offend God? The path from Susie's Cabbage Patch doll to the agonizing questions of evil is shorter than we might suspect. Did God say no to victims of the Holocaust? The problem of evil that theologians wrestle with has its origin in questions like Susie's and the answers given to her.

In a similar vein a child asked, "If I pray for Grandma, will she get well quicker?" The theologian answered typically: "We do not know. We can, however, pray in the assurance that Grandma's health is in God's loving care. But we must remember that we do not know the will of God."

Both answers—"God said no" and "We don't know God's will"—are characteristic of conventional theology. As to the latter, it remains troubling that at critical junctures in our lives, religious answers wrap themselves in the shawl of pious agnosticism: "We do not know." The defense of God on the grounds of our ignorance of God's will is disconcerting. For even if we do not know what or why God wills, we surely know that whatever God wills must be for the good. Whatever God's reasons may be, He answered no to our petitions, and that response must be good. "God said no" raises a dust of doubt. Did God say no to the astronauts of the space shuttle *Challenger* or to the citizens of Chernobyl or to the children of Auschwitz? Are the natural calamities we experience—earthquake, volcano, drought—properly traced to the "acts of God"? The momentary answer to the "doll" question that staved off the question produced a calm before the storm. Does religion believe that this is the way the world really works and that this is the way God works in the world? Is the will of God, known or unknown, the real reason or true cause of the tragic effect?

Susie's question is not only about God's reality. It is about God's justice. Is no a fair response? The ghosts of first answers cast long shadows. While the root problem of evil is discussed in greater detail in Chapter 6, I am here concerned with responding to the question, "Does God answer prayers?"

What does Susie mean by "prayer"? She has picked up the commonplace notion that you can pray for anything. If you pray fervently to God, prayer can achieve whatever the believing heart desires. It is therefore not surprising that Susie believes that she can pray for a Cabbage Patch doll or an "A" on her arithmetic test. How shall we responsibly teach her otherwise without frustrating her confidence in prayer or the tradition of her faith?

Magic and Prayer: Means and Ends

We must help her distinguish prayer from magic. Magic uses formulas, charms, and incantations that are thought to exercise powers that can influence outcomes. Magic is concerned with changing the external world. Magic's end is to produce results. Prayer is not wishing for results. In authentic prayer, as understood by the Jewish tradition, there are no shortcuts to results. Prayer is concerned with energizing the means so as to achieve ends of worth.

There are religious limits to prayer: we may not pray for just anything we desire. Susie may not pray for an "A." Not getting an "A" does not mean God said no, nor does getting an "A" mean that God said yes. To pray for an "A" is outside the proper domain of authentic prayer. What then can Susie properly ask for? She can pray for the means to achieve her desired goals. She can pray for the patience and discipline to study. She can be taught to appreciate that knowledge, not grades, is the goal of education, and of prayer. Susie is not too young to be taught the tradition of responsible prayer.

As opposed to authentic traditional teaching, conventional teaching is inclined to view prayer as magical intervention, a way to bypass the ways of nature. Traditional teaching battles against magical thinking, which ultimately leads to the disillusionment with the self and the world. A rabbinic teacher notes that "He who extends his prayers and expects fulfillment will in the end suffer vexation of the heart as it is written 'hope deferred makes the heart sick'" (Babylonian Talmud, Tractate Berachoth 32b). Magical thinking invites false hope and false means to achieve its ends. It denigrates human knowledge and the

competencies that are required to achieve the ends
desired.

Intelligent Prayer

Thinking is prologue to prayer. For prayer is based on
knowledge of what is real. To understand what is real is
essential for the realization of the ideal. In the Jewish tradition, one is not to pray when intoxicated or confused.
The liturgical world of the sane and sober is not the prayer
world of the disordered and inebriated. Prayer leads to
decision. Prayer has consequences. To pray wisely, we
must know something about what the world is really like.
The intent of petition is grounded in the possibilities of the
real world.

The tradition differentiates between reasonable and
unreasonable prayers. The first in the series of petitionary
prayers of the daily prayer book is a prayer for intelligence: "You grace the human being with knowledge and
give him to understand." Often we are not taught that
cognitive character of prayer, the authentic characterization of prayer as expressed by the Jewish thinker J. B.
Soloveitchik: "To pray means to discriminate, to evaluate,
to understand, in other words to ask intelligently." Prayer
is about this world, and it must respect the world that God
has created.

In addition, the tradition insists that to pray to reverse
the past is to utter a "vain prayer." The Talmud cites as an
illustration of vain prayer the petition that the embryo of a
pregnant woman should be a male (Babylonian Talmud,
Tractate Berachoth, 54a). That sort of prayer violates the
reality principle of Judaism: "Nature pursues its own

course." It is unmindful of the irreversibility of time. A prayer for God to alter events that have already taken place is regarded as an ignorant, vain petition.

What are the implications for the life of the worshiper according to such an assessment of prayer? Even though the past cannot be changed, the future depends on our response. We may not pray that an amputated limb should spring to life, but we may pray for the inner strength to deal with the loss. We may not pray for the resurrection of the limb, but we may give thanks for prosthetics. That we may not pray magically for a result that defies the laws of nature or that contradicts the laws of logic does not reflect on God's lack of power. It acknowledges the reality that God has created.

The philosopher Moses Maimonides in one of his rulings wrote that one who whispers a spell over a wound or who places a Torah scroll or phylacteries on an infant to effect some healing are "included among those who repudiate the Torah." They wrongly use the words of the Torah "to cure the body" whereas they are meant to serve as "therapy for the soul." Prayer is no surrogate for medical attention. Prayer of its own will not cure cancer. It may alert the patient to the curative powers and inspire the petitioner to devote his mind and heart to participate in the cure. Prayer ignites the fight for life.

The Petitioner

Why should we bother to pray if God knows everything we want? It seems superfluous to pray to an all-knowing, good and perfect being. What am I in prayer when God is all, when God resides in a totally other realm?

These questions spring from a master-servant model that raises God and lowers humans. Divinity gives; humanity receives. God acts; we react. God wills, judges, rewards, punishes, forgives, hears, responds; we praise and plead. In this vertical mindset, God up there, the worshiper down here, the supplicant is dependent on God's goodness and power. He can be either a grateful or trembling recipient of God's grace. The petitioner has little to do beyond asking. In praise or petition, it is God who is to be moved.

Given that passive orientation, the kinds of questions asked about prayer are naturally directed toward God alone. Does God hear? Does God answer? Does God respond? Does God intervene? Does God know my needs and wants? Is God moved by prayer?

Where in all this am I, the petitioner? Turn the questions around. Do I hear my own prayers? Do I know what I want and whether what I want is worthy of being prayed for? Can I myself answer any part of my prayers? Am I moved by my prayers? Who am I who lifts his voice in prayer to an Other? What are my power and my energy and my will and how may they affect the outcome of the prayers I pronounce? These reflexive questions will not be asked in the conventional prayer model where piety is expressed as subservience of the self to the Divine Other. They will be asked in the covenant prayer model where the petitioner views himself as an active correspondent of God.

The covenant prayer is not modeled according to the relationship of king to subject, or master to servant, or shepherd to flock. Covenantal prayer is a two-sided relationship of co-creators and co-sanctifiers. I am not a passive recipient of an Other's will, judgment, and act. I understand myself as an essential and active partner with the Divine Other. Covenantal prayer increases the potency of the Divine Thou, by raising the power and the responsibility of the human partner to answer prayer.

Covenantal prayer presupposes the dignity of the petitioner. When the Baal Shem Tov, the founder of Hasidism, was asked how one is to bow before God in prayer, he replied: "We must bend down but not too low and not too often. For in bowing too low and too often, we may forget how to raise our heads." A disciple of the Baal Shem Tov elaborated: "The psalmist declared, we dwell in the shadow of God. When we are bent over, the shadow of God contracts. When we stand erect, the shadow of God is extended."

Rabbis of the talmudic period were uneasy with excessive praise of God. "If a man seeks to praise God excessively, he is banished from the world." The rabbis restricted the heaping of praises of God in prayer, not to dampen the worshipers' adoration but, as Rabbi Jacob said, "They knew of their God that He is truth and they did not flatter Him. The praise with which Moses had praised Him was enough for them" (Midrash on Psalms 19:1).

Covenantal prayer is directed to God whose divine image informs the petitioner. The reflexive character of prayer is not an invention of modernity. Samson Raphael Hirsch, the nineteenth-century neo-Orthodox author of *Horeb*, informs us, "To ask for something is only a minor section of prayer." For Hirsch, the Hebrew word for prayer, *tefillah*, is derived from the verb *pallel*, which means "to judge." Prayer is a form of self-examination and self-judgment to correct one's ways. It is the self who is the target of prayer. Who is the self who is addressed through prayer to God?

The Divine Image Within: Covenantal Prayer

The power of covenantal prayer derives from the basic biblical affirmation of the divine image implanted in the human being. The pivotal biblical verse is enormously significant for the human-divine relationship in prayer. "And God created the human being in His own image, male and female created He them" (Genesis 1:27). This root idea forms the common ground of discourse between the two significant others of the covenant. The worshiper is not an ear into which orders are shouted or an automaton to be moved about by the will of the Divine Other.

In covenantal prayer, the petitioner cannot pretend that he does not know God or that he cannot will or act responsibly. Prayer is a way of discovering who we are and what we must do to know God. "Did not thy father eat and drink and do justice and righteousness? Then it was well with him. He judged the cause of the poor and needy; then it was well. Is not this to know Me? saith the Lord" (Jeremiah 22:15–16). The petitioner does not deal with a God who hides His moral intention. Human moral competence and comprehension are prefigured in the Bible's account of God's intention before deciding to punish Sodom and Gomorrah: "Shall I hide from Abraham that which I am doing . . . for I have known him to the end that he may command his children and his household after him, that they may keep the way of the Lord to do righteousness and justice" (Genesis 18:17, 19). Between God and man is a compact that enables prayers of dependence and acquiescence to become prayers of interdependence and mutual responsibility. Prayer is more than something to be asked for. Prayer is the constant search for the means of repair of the self and the world.

God Also Prays

"In true prayer, God is both He to whom we pray and He who prays through us." This arresting formulation by the philosopher Paul Tillich expresses the unique status of the human petitioner. We are blessed with the God-given talent to think, feel, and realize the ideals that reside in us as potentiality.

Bearing covenantal prayer in mind, how do we respond to the question: "Does prayer move God?" Prayer moves God only if we who pray are moved to respond. If we pray and do not hear, or pray and do not attempt to act, we become ensnared in magical thinking. If we expect God to move while we remain still, prayer becomes a form of telekinesis, the production of motion in objects without contact. Prayer turns into an operation of a remote control, a verbal surrogate for true work on the self, the community, and the world.

One-sided, vertical prayer leads to placing the entire burden of petition on the Other. To petition the Healer of broken spirits and bodies, while in the same breath violating the dictates of physical and mental hygiene, is a blasphemous contradiction. To pray to God who brings peace on earth as He does on high without lifting our voice or finger to struggle for peace trivializes the function of the prayer for peace. There is nothing that we can rightly pray for that does not make demands on us. The object of petition is to energize us to act outside the threshold of the sanctuary.

Prayers of Repentance

In a discussion of the particular nature of prayers of repentance, J. B. Soloveitchik argued a position that is exemplary for all forms of prayer including the prayers of petition. "The human being must rely upon himself; no one can help him. He is his own creator and innovator. He is his own redeemer; he is his own messiah who has come to redeem himself from the darkness of his exile to the light of his personal redemption." The petitioner does not ask of God to alter his human character. The twelfth-century philosopher Moses Maimonides wrote in his *Guide to the Perplexed* (Part 3, Chapter 32, On Repentance), to expect God to change the nature of any person would render the mission of the prophets and the giving of divine imperatives superfluous. It would render prayer superfluous as well.

The change of human character that prayer intends to cultivate addresses the divine image within the petitioner. The rabbinic imagination conjectured that God Himself prays for His own internal change: "May it be My will that My mercy suppress My anger and that it may prevail over My attributes of justice and judgment, and that I may deal with My children according to the attribute of compassion and that I may not act towards them according to the strict line of justice" (Babylonian Talmud, Tractate Berachoth, 7a).

Prayers of repentance confront the petitioner with the "likeness" of God that human errors have marred. Prayers of repentance reflect our confidence in our capacity to control our emotions, to create a "second nature" that will enable us to begin again. The goal of prayers of repentance is to enable us to declare, "I am another person and not the same one who did these things." It expresses our co-creativity with God.

The question, "If God knows what we need and want, what point is there to petitionary prayer?" reflects the theological rupture in its understanding the divine-human relationship. It is not God, the Other, who needs to know the secrets of our heart's desires, but we who need to know whether what we want is attainable and whether it is morally desirable. Moses at the edge of the Red Sea before the pursuing Egyptian charioteers petitions God to intervene. But Moses is rebuked by God: "Wherefore criest thou to me? Speak unto the children of Israel that they go forward" (Exodus 14:15). The prayer is misdirected.

Faith in the Other is necessary but not sufficient for authentic prayer. Covenantal prayer calls forth the faith to go forward. In the mysticism of the Kabbalah, the power of the worshiper to affect the power of God makes of prayer an activating agency. In the language of the Zohar: "From an activity below there is stimulated a corresponding activity on high. If there is no impulse from below there is no stirring above."

Both the mystical and rational religious humanism within the Jewish tradition energize the worshiper to act. In the Jerusalem Talmud, the biblical verse, "I [God] have brought you out of the land of Egypt," is transformed into the bolder reading, "I [God] was brought forth with you from Egypt."

Is Prayer Flattery?

In rabbinic Hebrew, prayer is called *avodah*, which means "work." The worshiper knows the flaws in the material with which he has to work. He respects reality in nature and in human nature. He knows as well that reality is elastic. Reality sets limits on magical thinking, but it does not deny real possibility. The aspirations of the ideal are real.

The ideal of David was in the marble before Michelangelo touched it. The ideal of the divine image is in the soul before it is touched by prayer. The worshiper is a sculptor who painstakingly carves his self after the divine image. Plotinus advised, "Withdraw into yourself and if you do not like what you see, act as a sculptor. Cut away here, smooth there, make this line lighter, this one purer. Never cease carving until there shines out from you the Godlike sphere of character."

Exaltation of God includes praise of our own spiritual self that yearns for actualization. Far from flattery in covenantal prayer, praise of God links divinity and humanity through the religious ideal of *imitatio dei*, the "imitation of God." Applied to prayer, imitating God transforms obsequious adulation of the Divine Other into the moral imperatives demanded of the praying self. When Moses seeks to know God's way and God's glories (Exodus 33:13, 18), he is enlightened by God's self-revelation. What is revealed are God's mercy, compassion, forbearance, goodness, truthfulness, loving kindness. These are the attributes of divinity to be humanly emulated. The imitation of God's attributes is the ambition of prayer. It insists that the ways of God are accessible to the human being and can be humanly enacted.

"How are we to understand the biblical verse Deuteronomy 13:5: 'After the Lord your God ye shall walk'? Is it possible to walk after the Holy Presence given that God is a devouring fire? It means to walk after His attributes: as He clothes the naked, do thou clothe the naked; as He vis-

its the sick, do thou visit the sick; as He comforts the
mourners, do thou also comfort the mourners, as He
buries the dead, do thou also bury the dead" (Talmud
Sotah 14a).

Praise of God exalts the ideal for our own spiritual character. Praise of God serves as the benchmark against
which we judge the conduct of our life, and, at times, even
the ways of God. The ideal of the divine may give rise to a
reproach of God. Psalm 44, for example, was recited daily
in the temple by the Levites to awaken God: "We have not
forgotten Thee or been false to Thy covenant. Our heart
has not turned back nor have our steps departed from Thy
way that Thou shouldest have broken us in the place of
jackals and covered us with deep darkness. If we have forgotten the name of our God or spread our hands to a
strange God will not God discover this? For He knows the
secrets of the heart. Nay for Thy sake we are slain all the
day long and are accounted as sheep for the slaughter.
Rouse thyself. Why sleepest Thou, O Lord?"

Covenantal prayer is neither subservient nor imperious.
It opens a two-way bridge on which I and Thou may meet.

CHAPTER THREE

Miracles and Revelation: True or False?

*A miracle cannot prove
what is impossible;
it is useful only to confirm
what is possible.*

Maimonides, *Guide to the Perplexed III*, Chapter 24

If there is no magic in prayer, what of the miracles in the Bible? How do we distinguish between magic and miracles? And who, in a scientific age, can believe in miracles? Menachem Mendel of Kotzk maintained that, "Whoever believes in miracles is a fool; and whoever does not believe in miracles is an atheist." Can we avoid the paradox of the rabbi of Kotzk? Can we believe in miracles without being fools, or disbelieve them without losing faith? Once again the framing of the question boxes us into an either/or alternative that forces us to choose between blind faith and Godlessness. To avoid getting caught in the either/or vise, we must consider how the word *miracle* is used and to what kinds of events it is applied.

Miracles are taught in religious school and celebrated at home at certain festivals to publicize the goodness and greatness of God, who cares enough about creation to intervene in history. Miracles insist that the world is not one-dimensional and impersonal. Miracles evoke blessings of personal thanksgiving; we are grateful. But miracle stories are also troubling. Did the splitting of the sea or the visitation of the ten plagues really happen? How is it that we do not speak of miracles today? Is it because the world today is not like the world in the days of the Bible? What has changed—the world, God, or ourselves?

When as children we raised miracle questions, our teachers were uncertain how to answer. So as not to appear disbelieving, they opted to respond quotationally, to offer literal citation of chapter and verse. So as not to appear foolish or irreligious, they added a "scientific" explanation of the miracle. They then found themselves entangled on the twin horns of biblical and scientific literalism, a dilemma illustrated by the celebrated tale of Joey.

Before Passover his father asked him what he learned in school about the crossing of the Red Sea. Joey explained that Israeli engineers had laid pontoons across the sea so that the Israelis could cross over safely. Later, the same engineer corps detonated the floating bridges and caused the pursuing Egyptians to drown. His father is incredulous and angrily refuses to believe Joey's account. Joey responds, "But Papa, you'd never believe the story the teacher told us."

All are caught between conflicting sensibilities. Usually the religious and scientific assumptions are kept on separate tracks. Whenever science and religion intersect, choices are made to avoid a collision. We impose a credible scientific grid on the supernatural narrative. Such heroic attempts to harmonize these opposing interpretations invariably fail. The collision is unavoidable. The naturalistic account cannot satisfy the religious intention of the supernatural miracle, and the supernatural interpretation flies in the face of science and common sense.

Supernatural and Scientific Literalism

Fundamentalists treat miracles literally. The outstretched hand of God, the rod of Moses, the turning of the water into blood, the rivers filled with frogs, the dust turned into gnats, the affliction of the Egyptian population with flies and the cattle with pests, the visitation upon people and beasts with boils, the covering of the earth with hail and locusts, darkness and the death of the firstborn—all these events are interpreted verbatim. Nonfundamentalists also revere the Bible, but they are uncomfortable with the implausibility of its miracle events. Miracles insult common sense. To give the text credibility, many nonfundamentalists merely replace literal scripture with literal science. In the course of making the miracle palatable for the scientific appetite, they spoil its religious sense.

In many modern rabbinic commentaries, the ten plagues visited upon Egypt are explained along scientific lines. The explanation recalls that between June and August the Nile turns a dull red because of the presence of vegetable matter; this is followed by the production of a slime that breeds frogs; when decomposed, frogs beget flies that in turn spread disease.

Such a "scientific" reading falls between the stools, missing the seat of our religious concerns. For if the biblical reports of the plagues turn out to be natural phenomena, in what sense are they miraculous? If a miracle is only a coincidence of natural events, it has nothing to do with divine design or purpose. At best, scientific explanations may show that the so-called miracle could have happened. But no scientific account of the plagues can support the religious claim that the alleged miracle was caused by divine intent. Not "how" and "what" but "who" and "what for" are demanded by those who question the truth of miracles. Are the plagues acts of God or accidents of nature? Is it serendipity or God's intervention that miracles demonstrate?

Belief in miracles implies faith in a hidden purpose working behind the curtain of history. Not science but theology is challenged to explain the divine design of miracles. If the miracles as narrated in the Bible are not literally the work of the hand of God, are we to conclude that their claim to be miraculous is false?

Getting Help from the Tradition

The postbiblical rabbinic tradition contains many sugges-
tions for moderns who find themselves caught between
the natural or supernatural interpretations of the meaning
of miracles. Many of the traditional commentaries focus
on the moral significance of the event called miraculous.
The concern is less on how it happened than on its spiritual meaning. It is not whether the event can be explained
as a natural occurrence or a supernatural intervention that
determines its miraculous character but what the event
signifies morally that determines its miraculous spiritual
character. Many of the commentaries, for example, find in
the episodes of the Egyptian plagues a moral drama of
poetic justice.

The Nile River that Pharaoh worshiped as a god is
turned into blood as a symbolic punishment for throwing
the innocent male children into the river to drown. The
land is filled with frogs because Heqt, the Egyptian frog
goddess of fertility, assists women in labor. The pharaoh
who is jealous of the fertility of Israel sees blessings of the
goddess of fertility turn into ecological curses. Similarly,
the darkness of the dungeons blots out the Egyptian sun
god, Re. Symbolic explanations flow from the rabbinic
moral conviction that, "Whatever measure a man metes
out shall be measured to him again." In short, the attention to the plagues focuses on their moral symmetry, not
their supernatural cause.

The attempt to naturalize miracles proves as counter-
productive as the effort to translate the metaphors of the
psalmist into scientific terms. "The sea saw it and fled, the
Jordan turned back in its courses, the mountains skipped

like rams, the hills like young sheep" (Psalm 114). It is not the disruption of the natural order of the world that evokes the psalmist's wonder but the trust in the power of morality in history to triumph over nature. Mature faith is trust in the spiritual purpose that transforms life.

Faith without miracle is perceived in the tradition as superior to faith that depends on miracle. "Dearer to God is the proselyte who has come of his own accord than all the crowds of Israelites who stood before Mt. Sinai. For had the Israelites not witnessed the thunders, lightnings, quaking of the mountain and sounding trumpets they would not have accepted the Torah. But the proselyte who saw not one of these things came to surrender himself to the Holy One and took the yoke of heaven upon him" (Tanchuma on Genesis 12).

Moralizing Miracles

Moderns have much to learn from the classic rabbinic interpretation of the miraculous. In the Book of Numbers, the people of Israel are punished for their transgression of speaking against God. God sends serpents to poison them. Moses prays for the people's life and is answered by God: "Make thee a fiery serpent and set it upon a pole and it shall come to pass that everyone that is bitten, when he sees it shall live. Then Moses made a serpent of brass and sat it upon a pole and it came to pass that if a serpent had bitten any man, when he looked unto the serpent of brass, he lived" (Numbers 21:4–9).

On the face of it, this biblical account contains obvious marks of a supernatural miracle. The miracle came as a divine response to Moses' prayer and amazingly saved those poisoned by the serpents. Yet the sages of the tradition do not acknowledge such a straightforward literal interpretation. They ask rhetorically, "Do brazen snakes kill or bring to life?" Instead they read the biblical story as a spiritual lesson designed to teach that "When the Israelites directed their thoughts on high and kept loyal to God they were healed, otherwise they pined away" (Talmud Rosh Hashanah 3:8). What happened to the brazen serpent that Moses made in the desert according to God's instructions? We read further in the Bible that the figure of the serpent was turned into an icon of idolatrous worship and that much later it was broken into pieces by the righteous King Hezekiah. For this dismemberment the king was praised, for he did what was right in the sight of the Lord (II Kings 18:4).

This rabbinic refusal to accept literally a biblical account of an alleged miraculous event is not unique. The rabbis deal with a similar episode recorded in Exodus 17:11 in much the same way. There we are told that Israel prevailed in its battles with the Amalekites only when Moses' hand was raised, but was defeated when Moses let his hand down. Instead of reveling in this biblical account of a miracle, the rabbis protest: "But could the hands of Moses promote or hinder the battle? That cannot be." Why can't it be? It is rejected because the story as it stands smacks of magical thinking. The rabbis explain the biblical miraculous event allegorically. Whenever the people retained their belief in God, were loyal to His word, and turned their faces toward the heavens, they were victorious; but when their faith flagged, they were defeated. In this manner, a supernatural account is transposed into a spiritual value.

Divine intervention does not disrupt nature. Therefore, the rabbinic tradition could assert that biblical miraculous agencies such as the manna, Moses' rod, and Noah's rainbow were created before they occurred in history. They were created on the eve of the first Sabbath of creation in the twilight (Ethics of the Fathers 5:6). We honor God's creation of an orderly and intelligible nature. The sages preferred seeing in the apparent aberrations of nature what the philosopher Harry Wolfson calls "a preestablished disharmony." Divine wisdom and goodness lie not in rupturing God's reign of universal law but in the reliability of the steady order of the world. Faith is not dependent on miracles. Miracles depend on faith. And faith, far from blind, sees life's deeper truths.

The Miracle Worker

The Jewish reluctance to interpret miracles literally has an impressive history. Both the biblical and rabbinic traditions are concerned that miracle working not infiltrate the faith, for that would threaten human autonomy and responsibility. The Bible itself is wary of the charismatic's sleight of hand. "If there arise among you a prophet or a dreamer of dreams and gives you a sign or a wonder, and the sign or the wonder come to pass whereof he spoke to you saying 'Let us go after other gods which you have not known and let us serve them,' you shall not heed the words of the prophet or the dreamer of dreams, for the Lord God is testing you to see whether you love the Lord God with all your heart and soul" (Deuteronomy 13:1–3). Not the medium but the message is to be heeded. Not the charisma of the personality but the character of the content of prophecy must be validated. The success of miracles and wonders is irrelevant to the truth and meaning of the message.

In the Exodus epoch, Moses' rod is the medium for miraculous events in Egypt and before the Red Sea. But some of the classic commentaries of the tradition demythologize the rod. According to one rabbinic commentary, since the Egyptians were convinced that it was the rod that produced the plagues and divided the sea, God said to Moses: "Cast away thy rod so that they do not say, were it not for the rod he would not have been able to divide the sea" (Midrash Exodus Rabbah 21:9). The rod itself has no intrinsic power. Indeed, when Moses later strikes the rod against the rock to force it to bring forth water in the desert, it is deemed a blasphemous act, though here too, the rod produced a miraculous event. Because of his abuse of the rod, Moses is denied entrance into the promised land. It is not the rod but the nature of purpose to which it is put to use that entitles an event to be raised to the status of the miraculous. Miracles to be worthy of the name must serve a higher purpose.

Miracles and Medicine

There were and are true believers who look askance at human natural invention on the grounds that such initiative supplants the miraculous works of divine intervention. The history of religion records many controversies in which the pious even sought to ban the use of medicine because such human activity was deemed to be an arrogant replacement for faith in God. If God afflicts us with illness, He and no other can and should cure the ailment. To circumvent God's will by human ingenuity denies God's exclusive sovereignty. For such people, true faith is gazing upon the desert icons of the bronze serpent. Only absence of belief in the miracle turns people to medicine and physicians for help.

Maimonides characterized this attitude as a perversion of piety. "If someone suffers from hunger and turns to bread and, by consuming it, heals himself from his great suffering, shall we say that he has abandoned trust in God? Just as I thank God when I eat for His having provided something to satisfy my hunger and to give me life and sustain me, thus should I thank Him for having provided that which heals my sickness when I use it" (*Commentary of the Mishnah Pesachim* 4:10). To depend on miracles is to belittle our divinely given intelligence as well as our moral responsibility.

Miracles and Wisdom

Faith in miracles is no mark of piety when it is introduced at the cost of disrespecting human intelligence and of mocking the reality principle. A key discussion in the Talmud centers around the claim made by some sages that people who are engaged in fulfilling a religious precept are never harmed. That assertion is challenged by other rabbis, who cite the contrary case of a son who dutifully obeyed his father who asked him to fetch some eggs from the nest in a tree. The son climbed a ladder, and, following the biblical precept, chased away the mother bird to spare her the anguish of seeing her eggs taken. About to return to his father with the eggs in hand, the son fell from the ladder and was killed. Where, the rabbis asked, was the promised protection for the son?

The severity of the question is bolstered by two scriptural verses in which longevity is promised to those who honor their fathers and mothers, and long life is assured those who dismiss the mother bird before taking the eggs from the nest (Deuteronomy 5:16; 22:6). In our case, the son was neither guarded from harm nor rewarded for his piety. Does God not keep His word? Rabbi Eleazar rose to explain the apparent contradiction. The son had chosen to stand on a rickety ladder, so his fall was likely. "One must never stand in a place of danger expecting a miracle to protect the faithful" (Talmud Kiddushin 39b). Faith is no protection against carelessness. Rabbi Eleazar goes on to note that the prophet Samuel, who trusted in God, would not go to King Saul initially though the Lord commanded him to do so. Samuel's reason for not obeying God is approved of because where injury is likely, one must not rely on miracles. "And Samuel said, how can I go? If Saul hear it, he will kill me" (I Samuel 16:2). Trust in God does not call for disregard of reality. Prudent judgment is an essential aspect of faith.

How to Teach Miracles Today

On occasion, the philosopher Abraham Joshua Heschel would open his evening lectures with an announcement that he had just experienced a miracle. He went on to explain to the puzzled audience that he had observed the setting of the sun. For Heschel, the miraculous is discovered through the faithful eye. It is not to be looked for in the strange events in nature but in the ordinariness of our existence. "To pray," he wrote, "is to take notice of the wonder, to regain a sense of the mystery that animates all beings, the Divine margin in all attainments."

How can the idea of the miraculous be meaningful to us today? We may be guided by the biblical Hebrew term for miracle, *nes*, which means "sign." Its Hebrew synonyms, *oth* and *mofeth*, in the Bible are translated as "signal, standard, ensign." In the Septuagint, the Greek translation of the Bible, *semeion* (which means "sign"), is used to translate *nes*. A miracle is an event that signifies something of "sign-ificance," something that makes an important difference in my life or in the life of my community. A miracle is an intimation of an experience of transcending meaning. The sign-miracle does not refer to something beyond or contrary to logic or nature. It refers to events and experiences that take notice of the extraordinary in the ordinary, the wonder in the everyday, the marvel in the routine.

Sign-miracles do not violate reason or nature. They are natural moments in our lives that we recognize as transforming. For many, the birth of a child is such an event. When a child is born, husband and wife are transformed into parents. They are no longer only inheritors but become transmitters of values. The natural biological account of birth does not compromise the spiritual significance. What is significant is the meaning of this newborn for the family, for humanity, for the world. With masterful irony, Maimonides described the bias of those who are blind to the "miracle" of the natural. He noted the absurdity of those who cannot see the greatness and goodness of God in the natural events and oppose scientific explanations as if they denigrated God's wisdom. Maimonides observed that if you explain to some pious sages that it is God who sends a fiery angel to enter the womb of a woman and forms the fetus there, they would accept it as a religious account of God's power and wisdom. They would marvel at the miracle that the "angel" is a body formed of burning fire whose size is equal to a third part of the whole world. But they would be repelled by the explanation that God "has placed in the sperm a formative force shaping the limbs and giving them their configuration." They would foolishly shirk from the idea that this natural force is what is meant by the "angel" (*Guide to the Perplexed*, Part II, Chapter 6).

The tradition refers to ordinary events that prove to be significant moments in our lives as "hidden miracles." Hidden miracles are all around us. A major prayer recited thrice daily is worded to acknowledge thankfully "Thy wonders and Thy miracles which are daily with us evening, morn, and noon." The signs of transcendence are discovered within the ordinary course of living. To see the divine in the natural and the rational, in the application of human intelligence and goodness, is a major insight of the Jewish tradition. The exercise of human talent, energy, and dedication and the course of nature glorifies God.

Rabbi Baruch of Mezbizh was asked why, in a popular prayer, God is called "creator of remedies, awesome in praises, doing wonders." Why should remedies stand next to wonders and even precede them? He answered: "God does not want to be praised as the Lord of supernatural miracles. And so, here, through the mention of remedies, nature is introduced and put first. But the truth is that everything is a miracle and a wonder."

Preparing for the Signs of the Miraculous

How can we sensitize ourselves and our children to the signals of divinity in the normal course of nature? How are sign-miracles experienced morning, noon, and night, as the prayer book states?

I cut my hand. The wound hurts and bleeds. I wash my hands, cleanse the wound, apply an antiseptic and bandage. Days pass and beneath the bandage a scab is formed. What can I learn from this prosaic event? I can pay attention to the natural healing process in my body aided by the intelligent application of medicines. Normal "miraculous" events are transactions between that over which we have little control and that over which we have a measure of control. It marks a partnership between the given and the transformed. Left unattended, the cut might have become infected. The washing, the medicine, and the bandaging are essential parts of the healing. Still, the scab cannot be said to have been formed by my will or wisdom. Healing exhibits a collaboration between potentiality and actualization, between the conscious and unconscious powers. Healing points to the human as well as to that which is beyond human powers. Curing is a cooperative venture between self and other. Who, having undergone surgery, is blind to the "sign" of healing?

The philosopher Mordecai M. Kaplan used the ordinary phenomenon of children's growth as illustrative of this-worldly "signs." Children enter the class at the beginning of the term. Their height is recorded. At the end of the term the children's height is remeasured. The children have grown. What accounts for their growth? Clearly it relies on the human care of the self, proper nutrition, exercise, sleep. The human contribution is necessary, but not sufficient. There is something beyond that accounts for the normal mystery of human growth. The collaboration of human and nonhuman energies is a factor that enters the miracle of growth. Height may be largely under genetic control, but someone whose chromosomes permit him to be six feet tall may never attain that height because of mal-nourishment.

Sign-miracles are results of human and nonhuman interaction. They entail the appropriate cooperation of the will, intelligence, and care, which themselves are manifes-tations of the divine and the potentialities given for us to transform.

The Miracles of Wine and Bread

The kinds of observations I have cited imply alternative theological approaches to the perception of miracles. They help overcome the commonly held notion that the mea-sure of the miraculous is in the violation, not the regular-ity, of natural law and the rules of logic. They help us see that we have something to do with the performance of miracles. This approach remains a point of great con-tention. Conventional theology is apprehensive of the human dimension in the religious explanation of mira-cles—indeed, in the understanding of anything that is reli-gious. Though an antihumanist bias predominates in the teaching of popular theology, it is far from the whole of Jewish tradition. We need to pay attention to those tradi-tional insights that do not excommunicate the human from the realm of the divine. The theistic humanism within the religious tradition has a critical bearing on how we play our role in ethics, ritual, prayer, and the miraculous. As the petitioner has a vital part in the fulfillment of prayer, so the person of faith plays an important role in perceiving and implementing the normal miracles in our daily lives.

Theological humor is as rare as it is revealing. One anecdote tells of a man stranded on the rooftop of his home, surrounded by floodwaters. He prays to God to be saved. A rowboat with rescuers comes by and offers him safety. He turns them away, confident that God will save him. A helicopter flies overhead and lowers its rope ladder. The pilot urges him to climb the ladder. He turns the pilot away, resolute in his faith that God will save him. The waters rise, and in disappointment the imperiled man protests to his maker: "I am a believing man and have always proclaimed my trust in you. Why have you, Lord, forsaken me?" The echo of the heavenly voice responds: "But my son, I sent you the men in the rowboat and you dismissed them. I sent you the pilot and you refused his help. Why have you forsaken Me?"

Faith is a way of seeing and a way of responding to what we see. The idea of the miraculous that excludes human action and reaction to events, like that of prayer that excludes the worshiper from the petitions, overlooks the divine presence within nature and humanity. A classic rabbinic colloquy expresses insight into the interactive human-divine relationship that bears upon the notion of everyday "sign"-miracles. Rabbi Akiba is challenged by the pagan Tineus Rufus: "Whose deeds are greater, those of God or of man?" Akiba replies, "Greater are the deeds of man." The pagan is surprised by Akiba's humanistic response. To provide evidence for his assertion, Rabbi Akiba brings forth sheaves of wheat and loaves of cakes.

Akiba asks, "Which are superior?" Unarguably the loaves of cakes excel (Midrash Tanchuma Tazriah 19:5).

Akiba's demonstration was not to raise man at God's expense but to point out the wrongheadedness of Tineus Rufus's split thinking. The latter presented Akiba with an either/or alternative. Either God or man, either the deeds of God or the deeds of man, are superior. This blinds Rufus to the cooperative relationship between God and man. Akiba's sheaves of wheat represent the givenness of God through the seed, water, soil, and sun, which men did not create. The cakes, on the other hand, represent the human transformation of that which is potential into actuality. The traditional *motzi* benediction is not made over the sheaves of wheat but over the baked bread. Akiba calls attention to the daily sign-miracles. Breaking bread is as miraculous as dividing the sea. Similarly, the kiddush benediction is not made over grapes but over the wine that is brought to controlled perfection by human hands. Wine, not grapes, represents the fullest expression of the holy, the transaction between the godly human and non-human nature.

Biblical Revelation: Did God Really Say?

*The literal meaning of the biblical words
may lead us to conceive corrupt ideas
and to form false opinions about God.*

Maimonides, *Guide to the Perplexed II*, Chapter 29

If prayer and miracles are understood as interactive events between God and man, what of God's self-revelation? Is the Bible the word of God or the word of man? Are the narratives in the Bible fact or fiction? Is the prophet a truth teller or a liar? These forced options are fed by a literalist approach that treats the word of God in isolation from the filter of human interpretations. It is a piety based on a conviction that the more literal the interpretation of a text, the truer the faith; the more symbolic the interpretation of a text, the weaker the faith in its truth. I shall argue that the converse is true and that literalism conceals the depth of the biblical text. Literalism counts the rungs of Jacob's ladder while ignoring the vision of his dream.

No less a traditional figure than the nineteenth-century talmudic authority Rabbi Naftali Zvi Yehuda Berlin maintained that the entire Pentateuch "possesses the nature and the central character of poetry." Consequently, one must be aware of the allusions and figurative expressions of poetry to appreciate the meaning of the Bible (Ha-amek Davar, Introduction to Genesis).

The classic mystic text of the Zohar similarly assailed the literalism that strips the words of the Bible of their symbolic meanings: "Perdition take anyone who maintains that any narrative in the Torah comes merely to tell us a piece of history and nothing more. Were the Bible a mere book of tales and everyday matters, we could compose a text of even greater excellence" (Zohar 452a). The Zohar further explained that, "The Bible has clothed itself in the outer garments of the world and woe to the person who looks at the garment as being the Torah." Hidden from the external literal view is the root soul of all.

Consider what the story of Noah's ark loses when it is explained verbatim. The literalist misses the profound moral symbolism of the Noah event and its implications for a postdiluvian world. The lesson of the human capacity for self-destruction is lost, as is the ability of one person to save the world. Focus on the literal account overlooks the profound implications for human existence in the Noah drama. After the flood, God reformulates the original covenant with Adam, makes concessions to the fragile character of man, and comes to terms with the limitations of human value.

How many young and old people recall the Noah episode simply as a fairy tale? "Dear God," Donna wrote, "Last week it rained three days. We thought it would be like Noah's ark but it wasn't. I'm glad because you could only take two of things, remember, and we have three cats." The literalism that counts the number of animals on the Ark or searches for its actual location on Mt. Ararat turns moral saga into fantasy. A typical comment made by a professor of molecular biology and published in a major national magazine attests to the persistence of literalist teaching. Challenging the truth of the Bible, and in particular the story of Noah's ark, the professor wrote, "Given the dimensions of the ark and its wooden construction, the first stiff breeze would have broken it up. Its capacity was only a fraction of what was needed for the animals and their food supply not to speak of their specialized requirements for housing." The professor and his religious school teachers missed the song of the saga.

The Bible is not a reporter's journal recording the who, what, when, and where of events. Finding the planks of the ark on Mt. Ararat adds nothing to our knowledge of man's religious struggle for a meaningful existence that is implicit in the Noah story. The meaning of the destruction of Sodom and Gomorrah, for example, is not found in the geological evidence that cities in the lower Jordan valley were destroyed by a catastrophe of nature. The fact that fires from petroleum and gas seepages are occasionally started by lightning in the area of Sodom and Gomorrah tells us nothing of the meaning of the Sodom and Gomorrah drama and its moral role in the culture of the Bible. The pertinence of the Bible story does not stand or fall with the scientific plausibility that the cities were destroyed. The Bible is not a book of science.

The Bible is not geology. The Bible is concerned with the spiritual implications of an event, not with its physical cause and effect. The story of Sodom teaches, among other things, that violence is self-destructive, that cruelty is contagious, that the end of the world is not God's doing but a consequence of human dereliction, that Abraham quarreled with God for the sake of innocent people and was not condemned for that challenge. Archaeology is an enterprise entirely different from the religious task of uncovering the layers of meaning in the scriptures.

There is hardly a verse in the Bible taken verbatim that is exempt from embarrassment. Take the statement: "And God said, 'Let there be light.' " If God speaks, does it mean that God has a larynx? In what language or dialect does He speak? Did He speak these words before the creation of the universe took place? How could light have been created before the fourth day when the sun and moon and stars in the firmament of the heaven were created?

Blinded by the literal text, the symbolic meaning of light and of the spoken word is invisible. Freed from the literal bond to the text, we may see that the sun is deliberately introduced late in the biblical order of creation so as to combat the pagan worship of the heavenly light. The biblical account of the sun and moon in terms of their function "to give light upon the earth" demotes the heavenly lights from their pagan status as gods. So too the creation of the world through the agency of a spoken word—"And God said, 'Let there be light'"—sets the biblical view in opposition to the pagan view that traces the origin of the world to violent battles between primordial gods. "God said" means that the world is not created by warring gods but by the word of a unified power whose intention is to create a universe of harmony.

Many children and adults are riveted to the literal notion that the human being is created in God's "image" and "likeness." Without appreciation of the depth of the biblical metaphor, we are led to believe that God possesses human features and emotions like our own. To deny the major role of metaphor throughout the Bible leaves us with naive images of God's nostrils, breath, hand, arms, eyes, heart, and flesh. Biblical metaphors taken literally compromise a religious tradition that struggles against casting God in the mold of human features and human emotions. Maimonides, among others, battled to salvage the biblical text from literalist reduction. Quoting the phrase, "If I whet my glittering sword" (Deuteronomy 32:41), Maimonides asked rhetorically: "Has God then a sword and does He slay with a sword?" (*The Basic Principles of the Law* 1:9). Clearly, he argues, such biblical expressions as "written with the finger of God" or "the hand of God" or the "ears of God" are adapted to the mental capacity of the majority of humankind, who have a clear perception only of physical bodies. Such metaphors "speak in the language of men." To teach the Bible in a literalist fashion is to leave religious people vulnerable to simplistic "scientific" diatribes.

To teach the whole of the Bible in terms of "true" or "false" judgments is to impose the wrong criteria on the scriptural text. We cannot properly ask whether the Book of Psalms is true or false any more than we can ask whether poetry, painting, and music are true or false. Books are written, art is painted, and music is composed for various reasons. Consider two books before us. One, written by an eminent ophthalmologist, Dr. Smith, discusses in scientific detail a complicated operation on Mr. Jones's eyes that has restored his sight. Mr. Jones also has written a book describing the same operation, confessing his fright, anxiety, pain, and then exultation after the bandages were removed and he could see. Should we ask whether Jones or Smith has written a true or truer book? Each book has a different intention and accordingly includes or excludes different perceptions. Some of the narratives of the Bible record a literal account of an event; others reveal the spiritual effect of the event on people. To treat the truth of the Bible as if it were all literal recording or all figurative portrayal distorts the multiple messages of truth. Dr. Smith's truth is not that of Mr. Jones. A single criterion of truth applied to both creates needless contradiction. Both are true.

Literalism and the Legal Tradition

The religious legal tradition has a special interest in overcoming the literalist interpretation of the Bible. The misinterpretation of the "eye for an eye" passage (Exodus 21:24), for example, derives from a verbatim reading. The rabbis in the Talmud argued against that literalism. Literally interpreted, the verse is reduced to absurdity. How could the "eye for eye, tooth for tooth" law be applied to a sightless person who blinds the eye of another; or a toothless offender who knocks the tooth out of the mouth of another? Literally applied, the law would be rendered inoperable. It is rendered applicable only when the biblical statement is interpreted, as the talmudic sages did, as referring to monetary compensation for the injury, pain, medical care, loss of time, and shame of the aggrieved. In countless cases rabbinic interpretation liberated the believer from a slavish verbatim understanding of the text. Far from getting closer to the text, a nearsighted literalism distorts the multifaceted spiritual meanings of the biblical word.

The Flaws of the Biblical Heroes

Aside from problems created by the literal reading of the Bible, many are offended by the questionable moral character of the heroes of the biblical revelation. The educator Trude Weiss-Rosmarin went so far as to say that much of the Book of Genesis is plainly unethical. What, she asks, can we learn from the first book and its heroes? We may well be upset by God's favoritism in accepting Abel's offering and rejecting Cain's; by the aggressive conduct of Jacob who wrested the birthright blessings of Esau through subterfuge and the provocation of their mother Rebecca; by the folly of Jacob's offering a coat of many colors to his son, Joseph, which initiated a cycle of sibling disasters.

Similar morally disturbing acts occur throughout the

biblical narrative. Was God's hardening of Pharaoh's heart fair? Was God's testing of Abraham's loyalty to Him by commanding him to sacrifice his son a moral act? Was Sarah's resentment of Hagar and Abraham's casting out of Hagar and her son Ishmael a morally just decision? Is visiting the sins of the fathers upon the children a right judgment? Given their behavior, are the patriarchs and matriarchs moral models?

Weiss-Rosmarin may have overstated the case, though the questions she posed are frequently raised. The questions are not impious and they are not outside the circle of tradition. They need to be answered.

It is unnecessary to defend each and every act of the biblical heroes. It is not Job whom God rebukes but the apologists for God who are denounced as "plasterers of lies." "Will you speak falsely for God, and speak deceitfully for Him? Will you show partiality towards Him, will you plead the case of God? Will it be well with you when He searches you out? Can you deceive Him, as one deceives a man? He will surely rebuke you, if in secret you show partiality" (Job 13:7–10).

Weiss-Rosmarin specified the unfair treatment of Cain after his murder of Abel. A rabbinic commentary anticipated her unease. Referring to the passage in which God accuses Cain, "The voice of thy brother's blood cried unto me" (Genesis 4:10), the rabbis reverse the chastisement. Abel's cry unto God is interpreted as Abel's protest against God's neutrality, not against Cain's violence. The protest employs a parable: "Think of two athletes wrestling before the king; had the king wished, he could have separated them. But he did not so desire and one overcame the other and killed him; he, the victim, cried out before he died, 'Let my cause be pleaded before the

King.' The voice of thy brother's blood cries out against Me." Far from apologetic, the rabbinic interpretation turns to question God's neutrality.

The response to Weiss-Rosmarin's critique is not to skip the difficult portions of Genesis but to read them with the courageous moral insights of the biblical tradition. The critique of God's role in history is within the Bible itself. Most people have never heard the protesting voice of prophets such as Habakkuk: "How long O Lord shall I cry and Thou wilt not hear? I cry out unto Thee of violence and Thou wilt not save. Why dost Thou show me iniquity and beholdest mischief? And why are spoiling and violence before me? . . . Thou that art of eyes too pure to behold evil and that canst not look on mischief, wherefore lookest Thou when they deal treacherously and holdest Thy peace when the wicked swallow up the man that is more righteous than he?" (Habakkuk 1:2–3, 13). The prophet is no yes-man. The heroic rabbinic tradition elevates the ideal prophet as one who defends both the people against God and God against the people, insisting on the honor of the son (Israel) and the honor of the father (God) (Mechilta, Tractate Pischa).

What of the heroes of the Bible and some of their morally questionable acts? Keep in mind that the Bible does not preach ethics in the manner of a didactic text. In the narrative stories of Genesis, the Bible does not telegraph its moral messages. The Jacob-Esau and Joseph sagas are moral dramas that must be followed to their conclusion. The Bible invites us to follow the serpentine trail of Jacob's journey. Emerging from Rebecca's womb, Jacob was born holding on to the heel of Esau, and later manipulated Esau to surrender the birthright. But the same Jacob must wrestle with his angel of conscience at the ford of

Jabbok, must have his name and character changed through his inner struggle, and emerge lame from the battle.

Jacob, whose career started in subterfuge, is in turn victimized first by the trickery of Laban who disguises Jacob's promised bride and later by the deception of his sons who pretend that the favored son, Joseph, was devoured by beasts. The postbiblical tradition does not spare Jacob criticism for usurping the birthright of his brother. In an empathic commentary, Esau, hearing from his father that his own blessings were given to Jacob, "cries out a grievous cry." Rabbi Hanina derives from this pained outburst a moral lesson. "Whoever maintains that the Holy One is lax in dispensing justice is grievously mistaken. God is long-suffering but ultimately collects His due. Jacob made Esau break out into a cry but once, but . . . the descendants of Jacob were punished" (Genesis Rabbah 67:4). God's memory is just; the punishment of evil is not escaped. Sooner or later we all eat at the table of consequence.

The Bible presents imperfect heroes. Without exception, they are fragile, fallible people in accord with the profound observation that, "There is no righteous person upon earth who does good and sins not" (Ecclesiastes 7:20). Moses, the leader of the exodus, is effectively deleted from the Passover Haggadah text and his burial place is left unknown lest it be turned into a shrine. David, from whose loins the messiah will spring, is depicted as a murderer and an adulterer.

The episodes of questionable morality in the lives of its leaders are not glossed over in the Bible. When Jacob, the father of twelve sons, doles out his blessings at the end of the Book of Genesis, he forthrightly informs Reuben that his natural rights as a firstborn are forfeited because of Reuben's infidelity by lying with Bilhah, Jacob's concubine. "Unstable as water, have not thou the excellency; because thou wentest up to thy father's bed; then defilest thou it—'He went up to my couch' " (Genesis 49:4). Similarly, Simeon and Levi are brethren whom Jacob denounces for using weapons of violence in their deceit of Shechem (Genesis 34). "For in their anger they slew men, and in their self-will they houghed oxen. Cursed be their anger, for it was fierce, and their wrath, for it was cruel; I will divide them in Jacob and scatter them in Israel" (Genesis 49:6–7).

The Bible: In What Sense Is It Sacred?

Given the fallible heroes of the Bible and even some shortcomings of God, what does it mean to call the Bible sacred? If by sacred we mean that the Bible is inerrant, its heroes infallible, its morality complete, then its sacred character seems questionable. But the Bible is holy not because it is the final word but because it is the first word of an unending tradition. Within the biblical text itself, there is evidence of moral change and growth. To cite one such dramatic instance, the self-revelation of God's thirteen attributes describes God as "keeping mercy unto the thousandth generation, forgiving iniquity and transgression and sin and that will by no means clear the guilty; visiting the iniquity of the fathers upon the children and upon the children's children unto the third and unto the fourth generation" (Exodus 34:7). However, the notion of inherited guilt and punishment in Exodus is explicitly repudiated in the canonized Bible. "The son shall not bear the iniquity of the father, neither shall the father bear the iniquity of the son; the righteousness of the righteous shall be upon him, and the wickedness of the wicked shall be upon him" (Ezekiel 18:20). The Jewish faith does not end with Deuteronomy. Its teachings are shaped by the conscience of its interpreters and are evident in the religious commentaries of its masters. The very text of Exodus concerning the visitation of evil upon children is lifted from the biblical text by the rabbis and introduced into the festival liturgy, but with startling changes. The liturgy recited in the synagogue today reads: "Keeping mercy unto the thousandth generation, forgiving iniquity, transgression and sin and acquitting." The rabbinic tradition boldly omits the phrase "by no means clear the guilty" from the prayer book. This omission offers further testimony of the evolutionary character of the collective conscience within the tradition.

It is noteworthy that the hardening of the heart of Pharaoh as recorded in the Book of Exodus, which disturbs moderns, troubled both rabbinic and philosophic commentators of the tradition. They recognized that if an external force, namely God, interfered with the Egyptian ruler's free will, Pharaoh was wrongly punished. In a far-reaching observation, Maimonides noted that the Bible often attributes actions directly to God while omitting reference to the mediating human and natural causes. Thus God may be said "to harden the heart of Pharaoh," but only in the sense that God is the ultimate cause behind all causes. God gave Pharaoh the power to choose, and that included the power to coarsen his own will and thereby to lose his capacity to choose rationally

and morally. It is not, then, God who arbitrarily hard-
ened the heart of Pharaoh, but Pharaoh who through his
own cruel habits forfeited the freedom of his choices.
Choice can be lost. Habits instilled in themselves by
human beings may create a second nature that distorts
the capacity to choose.

In what sense then may biblical heroes or people be
spoken of as holy? "You shall be holy persons unto me"
(Exodus 22:31). Rabbi Mendel interpreted this to mean
that the holiness of human beings should be human. God
has numberless angels; He has no need of more. Unlike
humans, angels have no pockets from which to distribute
alms for the poor. As a Jewish aphorism declares, "Let
your holiness be human, and let your human deeds be
human." The Bible, in Martin Buber's words, is "humanly
holy." It is written in the language of men and women
who are to strive to be humanly holy.

A rabbinic legend describes a dialogue among the
angels who are envious of God's gift of the ten words to
Moses. They insist that God should give the decalogue to
the deserving angels and not to mortals of flesh and blood.
There ensues a debate between the angels and Moses on
the mountain over the propriety of human or angelic pos-
session of the law. Moses asks the angels if they had ever
felt the desire to steal, or to commit adultery, or to blaspheme. The angels stand aghast at the questions. They are
flawless and without the capacity to sin. Moses continues:
"Then it is clear that this book is not meant for you. The
Bible is meant for errant, finite human beings who are
tempted to transgress."

Rabbinic legend further examines the fate that befell
the broken tablets of the law. Moses had allowed them to
fall from his arms at the sight of his people dancing

before the golden calf. But the shattered words of God were not discarded. The broken tablets were placed in the tabernacle of holiness to remind us that the sacred is not in perfection but in the struggle toward moral growth.

CHAPTER FIVE

Conscience and Religious Obedience: Is the Revelation Moral?

*The dilemma inherent
in obedience to authority is ancient,
as old as the story of Abraham.*

Stanley Milgram, *Obedience to Authority*

Abraham is ordered by God to take his only son, Isaac, to the land of Moriah and offer him there as a burnt offering. Abraham is a man of faith. He hears God's voice and is prepared to sacrifice his son. Holding the knife in his hand to slay his son, he hears the angel of the Lord "who stays his hand" (Genesis 22).

It is a disturbing story. How could Abraham agree to such a command? Why did he not protest? How could God make such immoral demands of Abraham? How did Abraham decide which voice to listen to, that of God or that of God's angel? Is God's word to be obeyed even when obedience can lead to the death of innocence?

Obedience to Authority

How does religion resolve the dilemma of obedience to authority? Is faith the triumph of obedience over conscience? If so what is the role of conscience in religion?

After the Nuremberg and Eichmann trials, the dilemma surrounding obedience to authority intensified. The standard response of those on trial was, "We followed orders." More atrocities have been committed in the name of obedience, religious or secular, than in the name of rebellion. The Nazi extermination of millions of Jews and non-Jews was carried out by ordinary people convinced that they were doing their duty.

Stanley Milgram conducted a study at Yale University in 1975 to investigate how it is possible for human beings to commit atrocities on other human beings. Was compliance to authority limited to the conditions of Nazi Germany, or can it happen elsewhere and in different circumstances? The results of his experiment are pertinent to our understanding of the ethics and use of the Abraham story. Is obedience the essential mark of the person of faith? Is this the point of the biblical lesson?

Milgram's experiment was designed to see how far people would go in following orders, even if doing so caused pain and suffering to others. The subjects who responded to an advertisement in the newspaper were divided into "teachers" and "learners." If the "learner," who was supposed to pick out the correct word from memory in an association test, got the wrong answer, he would receive an electric shock, from 15 to 450 volts depending on how many times he said the wrong word. Milgram asked several groups of people what they thought the "teachers" would do. Would they continue to shock the learner even though the learner was screaming and begging them to stop? All agreed that the "teachers" would stop.

No penalty threatened those who disobeyed, yet two-thirds of the "teachers" continued to shock the learners despite the crying and begging of the subjects to stop. The "teacher" subjects did not know that the "learners" were actors who were not actually receiving shocks. They just followed orders. Ordinary people doing their jobs, without any hostility on their part, became obedient agents of the supervisor.

Does Abraham's conforming response to authority properly prepare the believer to resist the supervisor's order in Milgram's experiment? We could object to such an analogy between Abraham's test and Milgram's experiment. Clearly, while the supervisors of the experiment were mere commanding humans, the voice that Abraham heard was that of the commanding God. That objection, however, begs the question. How did Abraham know that it was God's voice and not that of another that he heard? Was it God's voice or that of Satan that urged Abraham to slay his child? Satan's diabolical tricks include those of ventriloquism, the devil's uncanny ability to throw his voice into God's mouth. How do we recognize the voice that speaks in God's name? These are the moral nightmares attending revelation's claim to obedience.

A classic rabbinic text expresses unhappiness with the idea that God would demand the slaughter of Isaac. It goes so far as to conjecture that God did not order Abraham to sacrifice his son, but "only to raise him up" upon the altar (Genesis Rabbah 56:8). Abraham simply mistook God's intention. Some biblical scholars are puzzled by conflicting verses in the Bible in which the sin and punishment of David for his hubris in numbering Israel are attributed to God's judgment (II Samuel 24:1) while, paradoxically, another verse (I Chronicles 21:1) attributes the same sin of David to a judgment from Satan. Is it God or Satan who orders and ordains?

How are we today to understand the meaning of the Abraham story? We have choices from within the tradition. Two interpretations of Abraham's faith reflect two major, divergent views of revelation. Conventionally, the binding of Isaac confirms Abraham as the "knight of faith" whose fidelity to God transcends his love of his son. Abraham, on trial, has passed the experiment of unconditional obedience. In the liturgy as well, Abraham is honored for his willingness to sacrifice the promised future of his people out of trust in God.

From that point of view, what else should a believer in divine authority do but obey the directives of the voice? Surely we cannot evaluate God's intention with a human measuring rod. It would appear blasphemous to allow

God and humans to stand on level ground. "For My thoughts are not your thoughts, neither are your ways My ways, saith the Lord" (Isaiah 55:8). True faith excludes the moral judgment of mortals. Conscience cannot be allowed to contradict the divine imperative.

The alternative interpretation of the biblical account elevates the countermanding revelation of the angel of the Lord. On this reading, the angel who stays Abraham's hand is a symbol of Abraham's moral conscience. Abraham's acceptance of the voice of the Lord's angel over God's commanding voice expresses his faith in a moral God who could not will the death of an innocent. The philosopher Immanuel Kant would have Abraham respond to the voice of God commanding infanticide with outrage: "That I ought not to kill my son is certain beyond a shadow of a doubt; that you, as you appear to be, are God, I am not convinced and will never be even if your voice resounded from heaven."

On the surface, Kant's outburst expresses defiance of God. In truth it echoes Abraham's earlier biblical stance when upon hearing God's threat against Sodom and Gomorrah he challenged the morality of God's plans: "Wilt thou indeed sweep away the righteous with the wicked?" Neither the biblical nor the rabbinic tradition regards Abraham's rhetorical opposition to God's intention as a treasonable act against divine sovereignty. On the contrary, Abraham's dissent at Sodom and Gomorrah is grounded on faith in God's goodness and fairness: "That be far from thee to do after this manner, to slay the righteous with the wicked, that the righteous be as the wicked; that be far from thee: shall not the judge of all the earth do justly?" (Genesis 18:25).

The rabbinic approval of Abraham's confrontation of

God at Sodom is based on the moral covenant between them. Abraham is fully confident in God's justice. By contrast, Job's assault on God is considered less worthy than Abraham's because Job pleaded for an intermediary to intercede in the altercation between him and God: "Would there were an umpire between us that he might lay his hand upon us both" (Job 9:33). Abraham sought no umpire; he sought only God, whose justice would vindicate him even against God. Abraham appeals to God against God in the name of God. No intermediary was needed, and none could substitute for the God of justice.

At Sodom, Abraham learned that he was not dealing with an unknowable deity. The face-to-face encounter expresses both Abraham's courage and God's integrity. God does not wish to hide from Abraham "God's righteousness and justice" (Genesis 18:19). Abraham is explicitly given to know the attributes of God so that he may command his children and his household after him "that they may keep the way of the Lord" (Genesis 18:17–19). It is this knowledge that emboldens Abraham to dissent from God. On such a view, it is Abraham's knowledge of God's moral character that leads him to listen to the angelic voice of conscience that overrides God's command to sacrifice Isaac. Moral conscience is an internal revelation of the divine image.

Conventional teaching ignores the heroic role of moral conscience in religion. The rich sources in the tradition that dignify the role of conscience and its implications for the character of Jewish faith are untaught. The implication of the religious audacity in the character of Hannah, Elijah, and Moses, who "spoke insolently against heaven" and "hurled words against heaven" (Talmud Berachoth 31b–32a), and who are praised in the tradition for their courageous moral

dissent, are not as much as whispered in the class or sanctuary. The omission of such rabbinic spiritual material leaves
the false impression that the religious hero is simply an
acquiescent "amen" sayer carrying out orders.

Obedience to the commander is not always the proper
religious response. Moral sense and moral competence are
distinct characteristics of Jewish faith. Throughout the
breadth and width of the tradition, holy dissent against
God and in the name of God is a unique Judaic feature.

Religious Audacity:
Against God and in His Name

According to rabbinic interpretation, Moses rose three
times to contradict God, the supreme lawgiver, and each
time Moses succeeded in overturning God's judgment.
Not only is God's judgment reversed but Moses' objection
is praised by God and is itself incorporated in the law.
"There are three things said by Moses to the Holy One to
which the latter replies, 'By your life, you have taught me
something.'"

In the first instance, Moses interceded for Israel on the
occasion of Israel's making of the golden calf, an episode
that ignited God's anger. Moses pleaded: "Sovereign of the
universe, how can Israel realize what they have done?
Were they not reared up in Egypt and are not all the Egyptians worshipers of idols? Moreover, when You gave the
Torah You did not give it to them. They were not even
standing nearby. As it says, 'And the people stood afar
off.' You gave it only to me. You did not say, 'I am the Lord
your God [to the people] but I am the Lord thy God [only

to me].' You addressed me. Have I sinned?" Why shower the people with punishment?

God is not angered by Moses' defiance. Indeed, God is pleased with Moses' defense of the people even against God's initial judgment. God feels Himself properly instructed. "By your life, said the Holy One, you have spoken well. *You have taught Me something.* From now onward I shall use the expression 'I am the Lord your God.'"

Equally significant is the second occasion for Moses' dissent. In the Bible, the Holy One stated that He "visits the iniquity of the fathers upon the children." According to rabbinic interpretation, in the midrash Moses rose in opposition to God's words: "Sovereign of the universe, many are the wicked who have begotten righteous men. Shall the latter bear some of the iniquities of their fathers? Terah worshiped images, yet Abraham his son was a righteous man. Similarly Hezekiah was a righteous man, though Ahaz was his father. So also Josiah was righteous, yet Amon his father was wicked. Is it proper that the righteous should be punished for the iniquity of their fathers? The Holy One, blessed be He, says to Moses, '*You have taught Me something.* By your life, I shall cancel My words and confirm yours.' " As it says: "The fathers shall not be put to death for the children; neither shall the children be put to death for the fathers" (Deuteronomy 24:16).

Moses' argument is so esteemed by God that it is allowed to countermand God's earlier command and to be incorporated in the Bible. This religious tradition validates the right of the believer to challenge authority on moral grounds.

The third occasion occurred when the Holy One commanded Moses to make war with Sihon. "Even though he does not seek to interfere with you, you must open hostilities against him." Moses does not obey the commanding voice, but instead sends messengers to Sihon. The Holy One says to Moses: "*By your life I shall cancel My own words and confirm yours.* As it says when thou drawest nigh unto a city to fight against it, then proclaim peace unto it" (Bamidbar Rabbah 19:33).

Far from being considered acts of insubordination, these acts of dissent testify to the high status accorded to human conscience. Moses' moral assertiveness does not lead to anarchy. His objections are codified in the law and canonized in the Bible. "By your life," God says, "I shall record these words in your name" (Bamidbar Rabbah 19:33).

One further stunning rabbinic illustration elevates the status and function of moral conscience even when contending with divine decree. After seeing the dancing of the children of Israel around the golden calf, God addresses Moses: "Now therefore let Me alone that My wrath may wax hot against them" (Exodus 32:11). The rabbis comment: "Were it not explicitly written, it would be impossible to say such a thing. 'Let me alone' refers to God's response after Moses took hold of God in the manner that a man seizes the garment of his fellow." Moses, standing before God, says, "Master of the universe, I will not let go of You until You forgive and pardon Your people." God replies to Moses: "But I cannot retract an oath that has come from My own mouth." Moses responds: "Did not You give me the power to annul vows? Surely the law states that if the maker of an oath cannot break his word, he can consult a scholar who may then absolve him. God, come to me." Moses wraps a prayer shawl around his shoulders while God stands before him. Moses asks of God: "Do you regret your oath to destroy this people?" The Holy One responds: "I regret the evil which I intended to do against My people." Moses then declares: "You are free from Your oath. There is here no vow and no oath" (Exodus Rabbah 43:4).

Conscience, Covenant, and Commandment

While there is no Hebrew word in the Bible for conscience, its spirit hovers over the face of Jewish law and love. While there is no Hebrew word for religion in the Bible, no one would argue that the Bible is not a religious text. The acts and motives of spiritual heroes point to an intuitive moral sensibility that on occasion transcends the law or even the lawgiver. Far from alien to the tradition, the voice of conscience is rooted in the moral covenant between God and Israel. That covenant is reciprocal. It applies to God as to the people. One law in heaven as on earth establishes a moral universe of discourse between God and man. "The Holy One when He issues a decree is the first to obey it Himself; as it is stated, 'and they shall observe My observances, I am the Lord. I am He who was the first to observe the commandments of the Torah'" (Yerushalmi Rosh Hashanah 1:3). The God who voluntarily submits to the moral law is contrasted with the mortal king who decrees laws for others from which he holds himself exempt.

Conscience is the inner witness to the covenant that carries the divine and human signatures. Despite the apparent contradictions to God's word, conscience appeals to the God within God. Therefore, God registers no insult or anger against the challenge of conscience directed at Him. On the contrary, God recognizes in the holy dissent of the prophetic heroes His own truth. The rabbinic school of

Rabbi Ishmael taught: "Happy the disciple to whom the Master gives right" (Talmud Berachot 32a). Conscience has entry to God's appellate court. To whom else can the wronged turn if not to the God within God who is responsive to conscience. The religious figures who dare to confront God, protesting the unjustly injured, draw legitimacy from the divine source of conscience. The God within God acknowledges with pride the courage and the moral rightness of the one who seeks the heart of divinity. "You have taught Me something: By your life, I shall cancel My words and confirm yours."

The status and role of conscience in religion cast a different complexion on revelation. Revelation is not a one-way directive from above or a human projection from below. Revelation is the dialogue of reciprocal covenant, an ongoing process of listening and interpreting, of receiving and giving. Awareness of having entered the covenant makes it impossible to separate the divine and human element in the encounter of revelation. To paraphrase the philosopher William James, does the river make the banks or do the banks make the river?

Revelation promises the security and certainty of God's word. There are laws and statutes to be followed, customs and traditions that stabilize our lives. There is terror in anarchy and joy in the tranquility of obeying. But unqualified obedience has its own onerous price. The psychologist Erich Fromm noted the paradox: "Human history began with an act of disobedience, and it is not unlikely that it will be terminated by an act of obedience." It is with this irony that believers struggle.

Martin Buber recognized the awesome dilemma of revelation. Where there is conflict between God and the Bible, whom shall we obey? The instance that led to Buber's question was the biblical section in which King Saul is punished for sparing the life of his enemy, Agag, the Amalekite. King Saul acted out of compassion, contrary to the instruction of the prophet Samuel, who in the name of God commanded him to kill Agag. Buber wrote, "Nothing can make me believe in a God who punishes Saul because he did not murder his enemy." For Buber, the recorded biblical command has conscience against it.

In a similar instance, Buber's associate and friend Ernst Simon faced the choice of law and conscience: "Were someone to demonstrate to me that the oral law understands the commandment 'not to kill' as a prohibition against the killing of Jews by Jews alone, I would not accept the explanation of the commandment, and I would rely on autonomy." Conscience is the hyphen in the human-divine covenant that runs both ways. Conscience and commandment are not rivals but corespondents of a moral covenant. Conscience is indispensable for the moral sanity of revelation. It is not cowed by the sound of thunder and the sight of lightning. For if thunder and lightning are all that is needed to claim revelation, anything may be permitted. The test of the believer is not whether he believes or whether he obeys, but what he believes and what he will not believe, what he obeys and what he will not obey.

Conscience is no alien element intruding on the imperative of revelation. The divine gift of conscience exercises its moral sense and intelligence before saying, "We shall do." It insists on hearing first. Revelation is no buried mystery: "The Lord will do nothing but He reveals His secret unto His servants, the prophets" (Amos 3:7). "I have not spoken in secret, in the place of the land of darkness; I said not unto the seed of Jacob: Seek ye Me in vain" (Isaiah 45:19). Revelation must be filtered through conscience, which is the responsibility of every person who claims to hear the commanding voice. Conscience and revelation belong to each other. As the poet Wallace Stevens observed, "The mind that in heaven created the earth and the mind that on earth created the heaven were, as it happened, one."

Why Me?

*How can anyone of clear conscience
call good in the Deity
what he would reject
as intensely evil in man?*

Brand Blanshard

The angels grew jealous of God's intention to endow Adam and Eve with His own image. Should mere mortals be so gifted? They plotted to hide the divine image. Some angels proposed that it be hidden beneath the seas, others that it be buried in the tallest mountains. The shrewdest angel dismissed their plans. "The human being is ambitious. He will search high and low to find the treasure. Let us hide it within the soul of the human being. It is the last place in the world that he will think of looking for it."

The legend resonates with the theistic humanism found in the tradition. Much of conventional theology has hidden the freedom, initiative, and creativity of the human being. Yet the psalmist knew that, "Man is made but little less than divine" (Psalms 8:5).

The Limits of Humanism

Still, it is important to restrain the claims of self-sufficiency. In birth and in death we confront our limitations. We did not create ourselves. Part of the wonder of birth is the unknowability and unpredictability of the talents that may emerge from this protean being. In birth there is a natural awe and gratitude toward something beyond ourselves.

In dying, we experience a loss of power and a narrowing of choices. At such moments a terrifying lucidity tears at our autonomy. Dying, the very person who has been raised to the heights but little lower than God now crawls in the valley of the shadow of death. The self whispers with one of T. S. Eliot's characters, "I have seen the moment of my greatness flicker and I have seen the eternal footman hold my coat and snicker and in short, I was afraid." Out of such fear, our brooding imperfections, myriad irritations, petty anxieties take on new proportion. Out of fear, a greater appreciation of mystery, of the unknown, of the unpredictable accompanies the yearning for transcendence.

Along with the limitations of birth and death on the self, there is the confrontation with radical evil, so sinister that no mitigating circumstances can explain or excuse it. Helpless and hopeless the noblest aspirations of humanism are tempered. The wise preacher Ecclesiastes recognized the human limitations before cosmic forces. "No man has authority over the life breath to hold back the life breath. There is no authority of the day of death. There is no mustering out from that war. Wickedness is powerless to save its owner" (Ecclesiastes 8:8). Between the conceits of certain forms of humanism and the denigration of humanity in certain forms of theism lies the promise of a more balanced theistic humanism we examine in the following chapter.

The humanist philosopher Bertrand Russell criticized the shallowness of a pragmatic humanism that "binds on the surface of this planet the whole of its imaginative material; which feels confident of progress and unaware of nonhuman limitations to human power." Humanism detached from divinity proves thin, particularly when confronting the nonknowing of death and the misknowing of evil.

In the cavern of darkness, the cry "Why me?" cuts across all generations and all ages. Murmured or shouted, it is for many the straw that breaks the back of faith. "Why me?" "Why us?" Asked in different situations and in different stages of life, it clings to religion's Achilles' heel. The resentment or sympathy behind the question cannot be denied, and an effort to answer should not be postponed.

In a letter sent to Miss Lonelyhearts in the Nathanael West novel of the same name, an anguished young woman asks for counsel:

Dear Miss Lonelyhearts,

I am sixteen years old now and I don't know what to do and would appreciate it if you could tell me what to do. When I was a little girl it was not so bad because I got used to the kids on the block making fun of me, but now I would like to have boyfriends like the other girls and go out on Saturday nights, but no boy will take me because I was born without a nose—although I am a good dancer and have a nice shape and my father buys me pretty clothes.

I sit and look at myself all day and cry. I have a big hole in the middle of my face that scares people, even myself, so I can't blame the boys for not wanting to take me out. My mother loves me, but she cries terrible when she looks at me.

What did I do to deserve such a terrible bad fate? Even if I did do some bad things I didn't do any before I was a year old and I was born this way. I asked Papa and he says he doesn't know, but that maybe I was being punished for his sins. I don't believe that because he is a very nice man. Ought I commit suicide?

Sincerely yours,
"Desperate"

The question is not for Ann Landers or Abigail Van Buren. It calls for careful and caring attention to the question within the question.

"Why me?" conceals more than it asks. To begin with, the "why" in "why me" questions is not the same "why" as in questions about facts; for example, Why does metal expand when heated? Not all statements with rising inflections are requests for information. "Why me?" is a cry to be understood, a cry for recognition more than a call for cognition. *Why* means "woe." At the moment of the outcry what is called for is not a good answer but a compassionate response. A caring friend or a supporting arm is morally appropriate. In moments of such personal crises, theology is out of place.

Nonetheless, the call for comfort does not erase the need to respond to the intellectual and moral challenge embedded in the "Why me?" question. Emotional solace does not quiet the demands for an adequate religious answer.

Unpacking the Question

"Why me?" questions are peculiarly resistant to scientific answers. Explain to a relative what caused the congenital deformation of a child's feature or the fatal car accident or the death of a person caught in a tornado in terms of medical, police, or meteorological reports, and the facts will be acknowledged only to be followed by the same sort of questions. "I understand the X-rays, statistics, and scientific data. I understand how this event happened, but not why this happened to *me* or *mine*." "Why me?" is an outcry loaded with assumptions.

Here *Why me?* means "What for?" "Why me?" presupposes a universe of design in which the bad things that happen to us are divine judgments on our moral behavior. It takes for granted the correlation of human adversity and God's judgment. Typically, "Why me?" is followed by, "I have been good. I don't deserve this punishment." It opens a world of blame and guilt involving someone: God, Satan, self, others. *Why* means "what for," and *what for* usually implies "who." "Why me?" assumes a moral universe governed by a superior will with a purpose. Given these tacit presuppositions, the best scientific explanations that assign the tragedy to an accident or an impersonal natural event fail. The victim will assent to the facts of viruses, congenital weaknesses, mechanical defects, but only as surface explanations. The victim searches for the transcendent purpose of a divine Judge who designs and passes sentences.

We come across such transcendent purposive meaning in the concluding chapter of the biblical story of Joseph. Joseph's brothers, captives in Egypt, blame their sad predicament on their treachery toward Joseph. Joseph counters with a supernatural interpretation of the events that have befallen them: "And now be not grieved nor angry with yourselves that ye sold me hither, for God did send me before you to preserve life . . . and God sent me before you to give you a remnant on the earth and to save you alive for a great deliverance. So now it was not you that sent me hither, but God; and He hath made me a father to Pharaoh and lord of all his house and ruler over all the land of Egypt" (Genesis 45:5, 7). God is the "Who," and He has His reasons.

From this biblical view, what may appear on the surface to be natural consequences of human behavior—the sibling rivalry that led to the selling of Joseph to the Ishmaelites, Joseph's escape from the schemes of Potiphar's wife, his interpretation of the baker's and chief butler's dreams in the dungeon—is incidental to the purpose of the Grand Designer. Joseph doesn't accept a series of events flowing from natural causes as explanation of their situation. He offers a version of sacred history shaped by the hand of an intelligence beyond human comprehension.

There is grandeur in such a religious interpretation of the history of individuals and nations and consolation in the belief that our lives are governed not by natural causes but by deeper divine ends. At the same time, such religious interpretations when applied to our tragedies offend our common sense and our sense of morality. Are my acts, seemingly the results of my decisions, in reality echoes of another's will? Is the tyrant merely a rod of God's chastisement and his deeds only shadows of a divine will? Is every misfortune that befalls me or mine in truth a punishment for some transgression, known or unknown? Is every tragedy a moral judgment by the Supreme Judge who gives and takes away? Are hurricanes, tornadoes, earthquakes, drought, and flood truly "acts of God," visitations of His displeasure with an erring humanity? How then is the suffering of innocents, the torment of the ailing newly born, related to a compassionate deity?

"Who" and "what for" answers to "Why me?" questions open a Pandora's box. God's defenders spin endless apologies to explain away the seeming unfairness of events. Chief among their arguments is that God's ways are mysterious; His thoughts are not ours. True piety can only confess human ignorance of His secret acts. What mortals may see as evil may really be good in God's eyes. Who am I to judge the Judge of all the world? Like Job, I should be muted: "See, I am of small worth; what can I answer You? I clap my hand to my mouth" (Job 40:4). Once human ignorance of God's ways is conceded, God's defenders are free to multiply reasons for any and all tragedies: God tests us through chastisements of love; suffering is a favor in disguise; our sufferings on earth work off deserved punishment in this world so as to assure the joy of receiving the full treasury of merits in the world to come. The answers to "Why me?" are postponed for another world and another time.

Once granted an unknowable God, His defenders are free to mind-read the secrets of God's will. Given a God whose morality and wisdom are beyond human morality and reason, what we call good and bad or just and unjust are only the conceits of mortals. Once ignorance of God's moral standards is assumed, no possible fact or evidence can falsify belief. The suffering of the innocent and the prosperity of the wicked are resolved by a pious shoulder shrugging. Faith in God beyond moral critique carries a shield of invincible ignorance.

The mystique of Providence devastates moral comprehension. Who are we to evaluate God's design? Since God is good and wise, humanity must be deserving of its fate. It is the conclusion drawn by the God-defending friends of Job. "Think now, what innocent man ever perished? Where have the upright been destroyed?" (Job 4:7). Job's "Why me?" no longer needs to be answered. His moral competence has been taken from him. In the concluding chapter of the Book of Job, we discover a masochistic Job, made utterly subordinate. "Wherefore, I abhor myself and repent in dust and ashes" (Job 42:6). The earlier intimate dialogue between Job and God that rested upon a common moral discourse has been broken by a wholly other

God who will brook no moral dissent. The modern Job, however, does not clasp his hand over his mouth before the mystery of God. The Job I encounter is more like Martha whose letter I received before the Day of Atonement.

CHAPTER SEVEN

The Two Faces of God

When I judge My creatures
I am called Elohim (God);
when I wage war against the wicked
I am called Sabbaoth (the Lord of Hosts);
when I suspend judgment for a person's sin
I am called El Shaddai (God Almighty);
when I have compassion upon My world
I am called Yahweh (Lord).

Exodus Rabbah 3:6

Dear Rabbi,

Until this morning I have spent the High Holidays, if not in the spirit of fear and trembling before a God of justice, then at least in the sure knowledge that it is appropriate to review my actions of the past year, to give real thought to my failures and to resolve to be a better person and a better citizen. Until this morning I knew the central liturgy of the holiday well, but before this year I had approached it in an abstract intellectual manner. This year, I could not do so. Several months ago I had surgery for cancer, and I felt very keenly as I approached these days that in a real sense my fate for the coming year has been written, if not in a book of judgment, then in my own body. I look forward to health but I may not be granted it. As I read, the questions of the service were familiar. "How many shall pass away and how many shall be born; who shall live and who shall die?" But the response—"Repentance, prayer, and righteousness avert the severe decree"— for the first time carried a terrifying implication. It seemed to me as I read this that my own liturgy was binding my fate to my behavior, that my illness, seen in this light, has been the result of some terrible unknown transgression, and that the ultimate punishment for failure to discover and correct it could be my death.

I do not believe this—not with my head or with my heart. Nevertheless, as a committed Jew who takes language very seriously and believes in community prayer, I would be forced to repeat the central cornerstone over and over should I attend services for Yom Kippur. It seems today that my choice is a terrible one: to flagellate myself emotionally by joining my congregation or to spare my feelings by isolating myself from my family, my friends, my community. It is a choice I never believed I would have to make.

I know there must be others in our congregation who sit suffering silently, as I did today, who wish to join Jews around the world at this time but find the price too high to pay. I do not write expecting an easy answer; Holocaust literature has taught me that there may be no answer at all. I write instead because I must, because to muffle my sadness and my anger will destroy something in the commitment that I have worked so hard to build. I write with pain hoping that from the expression of my dilemma will grow some insight, some way to cope.

> With respect & affection,
> Martha

The letter refers to a major prayer recited throughout the High Holidays:

On New Year's Day the decree is inscribed and on the Day of Atonement it is sealed. How many shall pass away and how many shall be born; who shall live and who shall die; who shall attain the measure of man's days and who shall not attain it; who shall perish by fire and who by water, who by sword and who by beast, who by hunger and who by thirst, who by earthquake and who by plague, who by strangling and who by stoning; who shall have rest and who shall go wandering; who shall be tranquil and who shall be disturbed; who shall be at ease and who shall be afflicted; who shall become poor and who shall wax rich; who shall be brought low and who shall be exalted? But repentance, prayer, and righteousness avert the severe decree.

Martha is disturbed by the prayer. How do I answer her? Do I think that her cancer is linked to her behavior? Do I have a religious explanation of her illness superior to that of her oncologist? Do I trace her suffering to sin? Do I believe that the pain and terror and death are manifestations of God's "severe decree"? Common moral sense convinces me that there are misfortunes like Martha's that have no bearing whatsoever on the character or conduct of the afflicted.

I recall one of the first funerals I was called on to conduct. Before me lay a tiny casket, within it the body of a child. Was this tragedy a result of God's judgment? Had it anything to do with the child's behavior or the culpability of her parents? For me, the suffering of infants precludes any linkage between suffering and transgression. The correlation between sin and suffering contradicts the belief in a just and compassionate God. The High Holiday prayer, taken as Martha and many worshipers read it, describes a cause and effect relationship between tragedy and transgression that spawns anxiety, guilt, and dread with every illness and death.

Martha's letter calls for another theological approach to suffering, another approach to God, another understanding of the religious view of reality. What does God have to do with her illness? What is God's role in her life?

Martha's question challenges what we were taught about God's character. We could try to eliminate God from the answer, or offer her emotional comfort, or urge her to suspend her disbelief and cling to blind faith. But the root of Martha's question is properly theological. It touches on the essential character of God that affects the basic human-divine relationship. Martha calls for a belief in God that will not deny either the real or the ideal in God. God cannot be circumvented.

How can we speak of Martha's cancer—or the fire, earthquake, or pestilence referred to in the prayer—without reference to God? Martha was taught to believe that God is one in heaven and on earth. God is the creator of nature and the author of our moral commandments. Especially in monotheism, the problem of evil is crucial. For Jews, there is one and only one God and no other besides God. There is no Satan to fault for Martha's tragedy. God's role in Martha's anguish is inescapable.

God is real, the most real. God is ideal, the most ideal. And God is one. The root of Martha's question surfaces when the divine author of the ideal, "that which ought to be," collides with the divine author of "that which is." The strain of evil suffered by innocence threatens to break apart the oneness of God. Either God won't or can't intervene. Either God is not ideal or God is not real. Martha's conflict triggers the inner tension within ethical monotheism. How are the real and ideal to be reconciled and balanced? Martha speaks for a legion of believers shaken by the "unfairness" of life who demand a moral God not blind to the reality of evil. How can God's unity and Martha's faith remain intact in the presence of evil?

Two Names of One Divinity

God is One, but it is significant that more than one name of Divinity is used throughout the Bible and the prayer book. Two of the most prominent names of Divinity usually found side by side are Elohim (God) and Adonai (Lord). "Blessed art Thou O Lord our God." According to some rabbinic interpretations, God-Elohim characterizes God's justice, whereas Lord-Adonai characterizes God's mercy. The distinction offers clues to two major dimensions of Divinity. Deeper understanding of the dual aspects of God is helpful in responding to Martha's internal conflict of belief.

God as Elohim: The Religious Reality Principle

The God term, Elohim, first appears in the opening chapter of Genesis. In this chapter dealing with creation, the name Elohim is used exclusively. Elohim refers to the God of creation, the God of nature, the ground of natural laws. Elohim is the cause of the world as it is. Elohim is the God of the reality principle, the way things are, not the way things ought to be; the God of the laws of physical gravitation, not the laws of moral revelation.

The reality principle is basic to our understanding of the Elohim dimension in divinity. Its character is pronounced in some of the rabbinic discussions in the Talmud. One dialogue introduces a pagan philosopher who asks a rabbinic elder in Rome: "If your God has no desire for idolatry why does He not abolish it?" The rabbi replies: "If it were something of which the world has no need which was worshiped, God would abolish it. But since people worship the sun, moon, stars and planet, should He destroy the universe on account of fools? The world pursues its natural course, and as for fools who act wrongly, they will have to render an account" (Avodah Zarah 54b).

This seminal idea that "the world pursues its natural course" is reiterated in the following rabbinic discourse: "Suppose a man stole a measure of wheat and went and sowed it in the ground. It would surely be right that the wheat should not grow. But the world pursues its natural course. Further, supposing a man has intercourse with his neighbor's wife, it would surely be right that she should not conceive. But the world pursues its natural course" (Avodah Zarah 54b).

We know what is right; we know what is fair. But the world of nature is no court of justice. Were the world of nature truly governed by judgments upon our moral behavior, every natural event would be an ethical verdict: an earthquake would be a juridical sentence; a drought would be a punishment; a rainfall would be a reward; Martha's cancer would flow from a divine decision. The moralistic thinking that would identify nature's ways with God's will would engender a world in which demons reside in the lesions of lepers and benign spirits are found in the grains of the field.

Nature, which is traceable to Elohim, is morally neutral and offers no guide for human emulation. Nature neither validates nor prohibits thievery or adultery. Agriculture and procreation are indifferent to matters of legitimacy. From the events of nature we cannot infer the morality or immorality of those affected, or the outcome of natural events from the moral character of people.

The conception of God's nature called Elohim conforms with the view of the eleventh-century philosopher Yehudah Halevi. He described Elohim as governing the world "without feelings of sympathy with one or anger against another" (The *Kuzari*, Part IV, section 4.13). Elohim rules impartially. Elohim governs with moral neutrality. Elohim is the ground of Being or, in the language of the liturgy, "the life of the world," the energy of the universe.

Causes, Curses, and Consequences

Elohim plays a crucial role in sustaining Martha's faith despite the catastrophes that are enumerated in the High Holiday prayer she finds objectionable. Though every event has a cause that may be traced to Elohim, not every cause is morally intentioned. Earthquake, deformity, and cancer are explained in terms of natural causes and natural consequences, not in terms of divine rewards and punishment. Martha's DNA is neither morally praiseworthy nor blameworthy. It is neither a reward nor a punishment for her behavior or that of her ancestors. The part of the prayer Martha bridles at—"who shall live and who shall die"—is not a divine verdict, but a consequence of amoral causes.

The child born of addictive parents, for example, suffers as a consequence of that substance abuse. But those consequences are wrongly interpreted as divine decrees. A cause is not a moral judgment, and a consequence is not a moral punishment. It is a major error to convert a consequence into a curse, or to turn a natural cause into a moral design. As the rabbis said, "The world pursues its own course." In such a view of Elohim, scientific explanations of a tragedy do not contradict religious explanations. The oncologist's diagnosis is compatible with our understanding of Elohim as creator of all.

What Does Suffering Mean?

Do tragic events have meaning? Does suffering point to some deeper purpose? Conventional religious apologists tend to read God's value judgment into natural events. To them suffering is God's verdict. Tragedy is the result of an unknown divine decision, but one that holds the secret of meaning in His hands. They contend that people suffer for a purpose and that the purpose is cloaked in divine design. That logic is a legacy of medieval theology: without poverty there would be no motivating drive for philanthropy; without sickness, no spur to medical research; without pain, no cultivation of character and sympathy. That justification of tragedy still resounds in popular culture.

A well-intentioned statement of consolation declares, "At birth, deny a child vision, hearing, and the ability to speak and you have a Helen Keller. Raise him in abject poverty and you have an Abraham Lincoln. Stab him with rheumatic pain until opiates are needed and you have a Steinmetz." The Pollyanna comfort, however, yields a double-edged sword. What of the multitude of blind, deaf, poor, or tormented people who are unable to rise above their disadvantages? Do we rub salt into the wounds of those who did not or could not turn their adversity into triumph?

If not in divine purposive judgment, where can we and Martha find meaning in our suffering? We discover meaning not in the calamities assigned as "acts of God" but in the way we direct the course of nature through the exercise of our divinely given intelligence, courage, hope, and faith. Lightning that burns homes and fields may elicit heroism and sympathy, but the latter were not the intention of the catastrophe. The heroic response to tragedy should not be used to explain and justify its cause. When Elohim in the opening chapter of Genesis surveys creation to declare, "It is good," the goodness refers to the fact of being. To be is good, but this good applies universally to all of existence, to serpents and doves, droughts and waterfalls, cancer and chemotherapy.

Acceptance, Not Capitulation

Toward events over which we have no control, Elohim counsels a wisdom of acceptance. That wisdom is exemplified in the biblical account following King David's discovery that the child born of his adulterous relationship with Bath-Sheba is dead. David arose from the earth, washed, anointed himself, changed his apparel, came into the house of the Lord and worshiped, came to his own house, required his servants to set bread before him and did eat. The servants wondered what he was doing, saying: "You fasted and wept for the child while it was alive, but now when the child is dead you rise and eat bread." David answered: "While the child was yet alive I fasted and wept, for I said who knows whether the Lord will not be gracious to me that the child may live. But now that he is dead wherefore should I fast? Can I bring him back again? I shall go to him, but he will not return to me" (II Samuel 12:20, 22–23).

There are times when fasting, weeping, and praying are no longer appropriate. On our account, David's acceptance of the event as fact is not acceptance of the event as moral judgment. For that would mean that the punishment for David's sin is visited on an innocent infant and would implicate God in a moral transgression. The death of his son is no punishment for David's adultery. David must pay for his transgression with his own pangs of conscience, not with the life of another. David's acceptance of death enabled him to return to life and its duties, to turn toward Adonai, the other side of Divinity.

Lord/Adonai

The face of Elohim reveals only part of the persona of Divinity. Adonai is the other half. Adonai moves us to transform the givenness of nature that sometimes weighs heavily upon us. If the counsel of Elohim leads to acceptance, the urgings of Adonai call for transformation. While there are many circumstances beyond our control, there are within our power attitudes and conduct that respond to human tragedy. We cannot change the past but we can profoundly affect the future. When Martha recites the verse, "Repentance, prayer, and righteousness avert the evil decree," in the High Holiday prayer, she turns to Adonai, to the source of the ideals that help transform the givenness of nature into ideal ends. Transformation depends on human activity that faith relates to the inspiration of Adonai. Adonai necessarily involves human response.

The name of Adonai first appears when the human being is introduced in Genesis. Adonai, the source of transformation, is brought into play after the human being is charged to till and tend to the Garden of Eden. Up to this point, nature does not work to its capacities, both because the rain has not fallen and because the human being has not prepared the soil (Genesis 2:2). Only when the human and nonhuman elements are combined are the names of Elohim and Adonai conjoined. "Such is the story of heaven and earth when they were created. When the Lord God made earth and heaven—when no shrub of the

field was yet on earth and no grasses of the field had yet
sprouted, because the Lord God had not sent rain upon
the earth and there was no man to till the soil, but a flow
would well up from the ground and water the whole surface of the earth—the Lord God formed man from the dust
of the earth. He blew into his nostrils the breath of life, and
man became a living being" (Genesis 2:4–7). Not until
humanity is joined with nature is the name of Adonai
introduced and joined to Elohim. The Bible states explicitly that the name of the Lord was invoked only with the
birth of Enosh (man): "It was then that men began to
invoke the Lord (Adonai) by name" (Genesis 4:26).

If Elohim relates to the whole of amoral nature, Adonai
relates to that which human nature may do to control and
repair nature. Elohim is the source of the powers of nature;
Adonai is the ground of moral goodness. The rabbinic
mandate to imitate the divine—"As God is merciful, just,
loving so be thou merciful, just, loving"—is not modeled
after the character of Elohim, the God of nature, but is pat-
terned on the character of Adonai, the Lord of morality.
When Martha recites, "Repentance, prayer, and righteousness overcome the evil decree," she prays for the transformative powers of Adonai that help her mold the givenness
of nature into ideal ends.

Divinity includes both the reality principle of Elohim
and the ideality principle of Adonai. The realm of "is" and
the realm of "ought" are interdependent. They are not to
be split asunder. Adonai and Elohim are One, indivisible,
and interdependent, though they must be distinguished
from each other. There are roles Elohim plays that are not
attributed to Adonai. When, for example, a dying woman
asks for the meaning of her suffering and loss, I direct her
attention to the belief in Adonai that calls on the use of her

wisdom and energy. She asks what meaning remains for her, especially when as a young mother, meaning for her is in raising her children to be strong, teaching them to face the challenge of adversity. Now that death is imminent, all meaning has disappeared. Her melancholy confirms Nietzsche's aphorism: "He who has a 'why' to live can bear almost any 'how.'" This mother has lost her "why." Here the Adonai dimension of faith is crucial. She found meaning in teaching her children how to cope with life's challenges. I tell her: "Your children know how sick you are. In your sickness you teach them lessons that will sustain them the rest of their lives. You teach them how to love, how to cling to appropriate faith. Living you teach and dying you also teach."

This woman's faith and courage are transmitted to her friends and family. That is her discovered meaning. A rabbinic legend concludes: "The righteous are informed of the day of their death so that they may hand the crown to their children." To accept and transcend tragedy is to hold in one's grasp the power and goodness of Elohim and Adonai.

Transformation

Acceptance and transformation are basic responses to life rooted in the dual character of divinity. The daunting test of faith lies in determining when acceptance is appropriate and when it is premature. When are we to turn to Elohim and when are we to turn to Adonai? To cope with life spiritually is to know which events to accept and which events to transcend and transform. When King David heard of the death of his child, acceptance was appropriate. But so long as the child held the breath of life, he would not do so.

We illustrate the transformative power of faith and hope in the biblical episode of another king and his confrontation with the prophet Isaiah. When King Hezekiah was ill, Isaiah was summoned by God to approach the king's bedside. Isaiah told him: "Set thy house in order for thou shalt die and not live" (II Kings 20:1). The king was angered and responded: "Finish your prophecy and go, for I have this tradition from the house of my ancestor that even if a sharp sword rests upon a man's neck, he should not desist from prayer." Hezekiah turned his face from Isaiah to the wall and prayed to the Lord.

A rabbinic comment on Hezekiah's response to the prophet elaborates on the king's rebuke: "It is customary that a person when visiting the sick should say, 'May mercy be shown upon you from heaven.' When the physician comes, he tells the sick, eat this and do not eat that, drink this and do not drink that. Even when he sees him near death, he does not say to him, 'Set thy house in order,' because this might upset him. You however tell me, 'Set thy house in order for thou shalt die and not live.' I pay no attention to what you say nor will I listen to your advice. I hold on to nothing else than what my ancestor said. For through the multitude of dreams and vanities there are also many words, but fear thou God" (Ecclesiastes Rabbah 5:6).

The very prophet who prophesied Hezekiah's imminent death is told by God to inform the king that the Lord has heard his prayer and seen his tears and has added fifteen years to his life (II Kings 20:5–6). Hezekiah triumphed over Isaiah's doomsday prophecy and sang a prayer of recovery: "Truly it was for my good that I had such great bitterness. You [God] saved my life from the pit of destruction, for You have cast behind Your back all my offenses" (Ecclesiastes Rabbah 5:6).

After his son's death, David rent his garments, mourned his loss, and recited his acceptance. Prior to the child's death, acceptance would be inappropriate. But Hezekiah, although dangerously ill, was not dead. There were options open to him, and it was right for him not to cave in to Isaiah's judgment even though that judgment was offered at God's bequest. Hezekiah called on the transformative powers of Adonai within.

Asked to define the essence of wisdom, the poet Robert Frost answered: "True wisdom is the ability to act when it is necessary on the basis of incomplete information." The hope that Hezekiah manifested relates to the transformative powers of Adonai within and between human beings. Hezekiah's hope was not optimism. A distinction between hope and optimism is offered by the sociologist Christopher Lasch. Optimism presumes the inevitable progress in life, the sure victory of goodness, whereas hope is fully aware of the moral regressions in history and life's tragic dimension. Optimism claims evolution to be automatically on its side. Hope is more like the virtue of faith. Faith is not the irrepressible optimism of Pollyanna but the measured wisdom of what the psychoanalyst Erik Erikson called "the favorable ratio of basic trust over distrust."

Faith entails hope and trust. According to a talmudic parable, forty-nine of the fifty doors of understanding were opened to Moses. When asked how Moses could continue without the fiftieth door, he was told, "Seeing that it was closed to him, Moses substituted faith." Wisdom calls upon acceptance and transformation. Both are appropriate responses depending on the situation and circumstances.

King Hezekiah's trust and hope in the curative power of life have filtered down into Jewish folk stories. One such story tells of a poor man who is gathering sticks of wood in the forest. He packs them in a torn sack, throws the sack over his shoulders, and then stumbles. The sticks scatter to the earth. Frustrated, he cries out to God, "Send me the angel of death and take me from this earth for I am sick and full of sorrow." His prayer is promptly answered, and before him appears the angel of death, asking, "Did you call for me?" "Yes yes," stammers the man, wondering now how he can retreat. "Could you help me gather up these sticks?" However difficult our lot, life and health are sacred and worth struggling for. "For a one-day-old child who is ill," the sages taught, "the Sabbath may be violated; for a King David deceased, it may not be desecrated" (Talmud Shabbat 151b).

The Unity of God and Lord: Elohim and Adonai Are One

At the root of the sufferer's spiritual despair is the sundering of the Divinity of God. The real and the ideal in Divinity appear broken. Twice daily the Jewish tradition calls for the recitation of the prayer of God's unity: "Hear O Israel. The Lord our God, the Lord is one" (Deuteronomy 6:4). On the Day of Atonement, the culminating prayer declaring God's unity is repeated seven times: "The Lord is God" (I Kings 18:39). Each benediction unites Lord and God: "Blessed are Thou O Lord our God." The two dimensions of divinity belong together: Elohim, the God of nature, and Adonai, the Lord of morality; Elohim, the God of necessity, and Adonai, the Lord of possibility; Elohim, the God of what is, and Adonai, the Lord of what ought to be; Elohim, the God of acceptance, and Adonai, the God of transformation.

Their unity embraces the oneness of reality. "Ought" is as real as "is." Without Elohim, the ideals of Adonai are fantasies. Without Adonai, reality is robbed of the real possibility of change. To live with Elohim alone is to know nature without the powers to repair the world as given. To live with Adonai alone is to live by dreams without the hands and feet of reality. The traditional benediction joins Elohim and Adonai.

How does such a reality-based theology relate to Martha's conflict? The Jewish reality principle encourages Martha to confront her sickness without denial and without guilt. Cancer is real, but it is not punishment. Cancer is real, but it does not signal resignation. Cancer is real, but it is not always the last word.

The theology that calls attention to the transaction between the ideal and the real supports Martha's struggle to cope with tragedy. Creation is not complete. Everything created during the six days of creation needs work: "The mustard seed needs to be sweetened, the lupine needs to be soaked in water, the wheat needs to be ground and the human being needs to be repaired" (Midrash Tanchuma: Tazriah 5). Nature and its cultivation, creation, and repair are rooted in the reality of one God of two complementary qualities. Confronting adversity, Martha needs to recognize the wisdom and strength of both. The wisdom in faith lies in recognizing the boundaries both of the real and the ideal. There is a time to accept and a time to reject, a time for waiting and a time for acting, a time for speaking and a time for keeping silent.

The first principle of medicine is to do no harm; the same applies to theology. No theology rooted in reality can be expected to transform tragedy into joys. But no theology should pour the salt of self-recrimination and blame on the wounds of those who suffer. At the very least, theology ought not turn divinity into a punitive power or piety into masochism.

Checking the Excesses of Will

The face of Elohim serves to balance the excesses of human will. This is particularly important in a secular society that tends to exaggerate the role of human will. That magnification of will counsels Martha, in the face of her sickness, to grit her teeth and will her own recovery. Will has its place but it needs limits.

Symptomatic of secular "willism" are the testimonies of the curative powers of the will to triumph over sickness. One such best-selling book, *Love, Medicine and Miracles*, written by an oncological surgeon, Bernie Siegel, describes numerous miraculous recoveries from illnesses in defiance of the gloomy prognostications of medical experts. He cites accounts of "exceptional patients" who will not go quietly onto the gurney. These are the so-called bad patients, whose will to triumph over illness has turned victims into victors. In *Peace, Love and Healing*, Siegel quotes a novelist: "Illness doesn't strike randomly like a thief in the night. Certain kinds of people at certain points in their lives will come down with certain ailments. You can almost predict it."

Such counsel places an inordinate trust in human will both to avoid and overcome illnesses. It proffers an unlimited optimism that frequently boomerangs on the believer. If "Why me?" searches for a "who" that it traces to God's will, this bravado identifies the "who" in the patient himself. The self takes the place of God, and with this a number of unsatisfactory consequences follow.

Exaggerated self-assertion is the dominant mood of this secular optimism. In the language of a psychologist cited in Siegel's book: "I am me. Therefore everything that comes out of me is authentically mine because I alone chose it. I own everything about me, my body, my mind, my eyes. I own my fantasies, my dreams, my fears, my triumphs, my failures, my mistakes. I own me and therefore I can engineer me. I am me and I am okay." We may appreciate the assertiveness of self and the refusal to blame others for things that affect us. At the same time, we must be wary of the negative consequences of such willfulness. Given the virtual omnipotence of the self, there is no one to blame for Martha's cancer except herself, and there is no one to blame for the failure to recover except her own self. She faces double jeopardy. Contraction of an illness and failure to recover are seen as evidence of twin failures of the will.

If conventional theology tends to accuse the sinner as the cause of her suffering, this form of willful optimism blames the patient for her failure to act like the recovering "exceptional patients." One patient, after reading the literature concerning exceptional patients, cried, "What's wrong with me? I have tried. God knows, I have tried. I have gritted my teeth. I have taken my chemotherapy. I have given and received love. Why can't I will myself into wellness like those others?"

Soldiers who return from war while their comrades lie on the battlefield often report survivor guilt: "Why did I live while the others died?" Ordinary patients who hear of "exceptional patients" whose attitude helped them triumph over their sickness report what may be called victim guilt: "Why do they deserve recovery and not me?"

What is lacking in this hyperbolic optimism is a balanced view of the ideality of Adonai and the reality of Elohim. The prudent voice of Elohim is needed to temper the exaggerated confidence in the omnipotence of the human will. Elohim is needed to avoid the false self-recrimination that follows from excessive faith in the power of human will.

We are raised to believe that will revives, redeems, and cures. Here the acceptance of the reality principle of Elohim is important to restrain the intoxicated ambition of human will. The religious reality principle informs the patient that just as cancer is not the result of God's will neither is the lack of recovery the result of the absence of human will. Human will is not omnipotent. Some things can be willed; others cannot. Smiling can be willed; happiness cannot. Eating can be willed; hunger cannot. Reading prayers can be willed; belief cannot. Taking chemotherapy can be willed, not the remission of the illness.

Given the distinctions between Elohim and Adonai, there is an answer to Martha's demand for an explanation of the prayer, "How many shall pass away and how many shall die." The catastrophes mentioned in this part of the prayer refer to what philosophers call "natural evil," the events beyond human intention and control. The causes of these are morally neutral. Theologically they may be ascribed to God as Elohim, the God of nature. But what of the moral evils that originate in human beings? There are intentionally caused moral evils over which we do exercise control and for which we own responsibility, including the obligation to repair the injury caused. When we turn away from our capacity to repent and repair, we turn from Adonai. "Repentance, prayer, and acts of charity" are spiritual capacities, and their use or abandonment are in our hands.

Martha's cancer is fault-free. It is not a sentence of God. It is not the product of will or a failure of will, hers or God's.

The Two Faces of Human Nature: Good and Evil Inclinations

There is a duality of self that reflects the two dimensions of God. The human being, according to the Jewish tradition, is possessed by two basic inclinations. One is called *yetzer hatov,* the good disposition that is credited with moral choices. The other is called *yetzer hara,* usually translated as evil inclination and most often associated with sexual temptation. But the meaning of *yetzer hara* is closer to the idea of a neutral energy akin to the libido. The so-called evil inclination is like electricity, an energy that can be used to light the darkness or to start a fire. It can be used to consecrate or desecrate the self or the other.

Like Elohim and Adonai, the two human inclinations are not in conflict. There is no devil in human nature any more than there is a Satan in the nature of Divinity. Both good and evil have a common source in one God who "forms light and creates darkness, makes peace and creates evil" (Isaiah 45:7). The so-called evil inclination, according to a rabbinic passage, is "joined with mercy and envy as three good qualities created in this world" (Fathers of Rabbi Nathan 9a). The tradition doesn't urge the extirpation of the evil impulse, only its sublimation.

In a profound talmudic myth, the evil inclination is described as a young, fiery lion coming forth from the Holy of Holies. It is seized hold of and imprisoned by the sages for three days. But during this period of the incarceration, the sages "looked in the whole land for a fresh egg and could not find it" (Talmud Yoma 69b). Without the libido, the joy of life is taken from this world. Without the presence of the evil inclination, there would be no civilization. As the rabbis pointed out: "Were it not for the evil inclination a man would not build a house or take a wife or beget children or engage in business" (Genesis Rabbah 9:7). The sages faced a taunting dilemma. What shall they do with the evil inclination now that it is imprisoned? To kill the evil inclination would be tantamount to destroying the world. Yet to free the evil inclination would allow its mischief to roam free.

The rabbis counseled together and decided that they would pray to God for "half mercy." They would, as it were, divide their prayer. Let the libido of the evil temptation be preserved, but let it be limited to lawful acts. Let lust exist, but let it be restricted to one's spouse. Let competition prevail, but let it be limited to legitimate businesses. The perceptive answer the rabbis receive informs them that, "Half measures are not granted from heaven" (Talmud Yoma ibid.). The real world does not come compartmentalized, neatly packaged into separate parts marked "good" or "bad." But within the larger realm of neutral energies, the human being possesses the power to sanctify or to desecrate. Monotheism requires of its believers the wisdom of differentiation, the exercise of moral choice.

The human image mirrors the complementary features of Elohim and Adonai which, when held in balance, reflect the ideal of monotheism. The *yetzer hara,* the totality of our inclinations, instincts, drives, and impulses, is not to be rejected or crushed. It is to be controlled and sublimated by the good inclination and integrated into the self.

A Personal Answer to Martha

There is a better time and place to speak theology than in the hospital or mortuary. The clarification of faith should come earlier, in calmer, healthier times, during the formative years of our lives. Still one cannot always choose the ideal time and place to anticipate the crises of faith in our lives. Martha questions me now and here. In response to Martha and those who, like her, find themselves in extreme situations, I have discussed a theological approach that I may summarize in more personal terms.

I do not believe that sickness is a divine punishment, a malediction thrust down upon me from above, a chastisement meant to correct some transgression, a mysterious test of my strength or weakness.

"Nature pursues its own course," the Sages declared independent of my doing or intent, a flow of events falling indiscriminately upon young and old, good or bad.

Flowers wither, leaves fall, the earth cracks open, none the result of a supernal judging God, but of Elohim, the mother of the universe, creator of lion and lamb, eagle and dove, and all the ways of earth.

Where in this ailing is Adonai to be found? Adonai is in the petitions for courage and hope. Adonai is in the curative forces I cannot locate but discover within me and between us. Adonai is in the healing powers that form scars closing lesions, in the life-sustaining energies brought forth by men and women, doctors, nurses, family, and friends who stand beside my bed, hold my hand, bless me with their prayers. Their energies move me with a desire to recover, to struggle for my health. I sense the divine forces within and without, between the conscious and the unconscious of my self.

I need them both, Adonai, the source of healing, and Elohim, the life of the universe. Adonai/Elohim, reflections of the unity we yearn for to make us whole. Adonai/Elohim, the harmony we seek to accept and transform.

Adonai/Elohim reminds me that it is never too late to alter my world, not by magic incantations or manipulations of the cards but by faith-wisdom to open myself to the curative forces I cannot always define but can feel surge within me. In sickness and in dying, it is never too late. Living I teach, dying I teach. Others I love learn from my bearing, my posture. Blessed is Adonai/Elohim who has created within us the promise of your united image.

In the Wake of the Northridge Earthquake

Not long after I wrote the above, the Richter scale recorded 6.6 and my community was shaken with the dybbuk-like fury of the Northridge earthquake. The children of the religious school were gathered in a series of assemblies to enable them to ventilate their fears in a friendly setting. In all the assemblies with children of all ages the same question reappeared: "Why was God angry with us?" The parents asked much the same question. They wanted to know whether this random destruction of Los Angeles was "an act of God." They wished to know why it happened here and now and to them.

Why Los Angeles and not New York? These questions from anguished people were refrains of the kind of concerns expressed in Europe after the Lisbon earthquake of 1755. Why Lisbon and not London or Paris? The premise of these questions assumed that this natural catastrophe could not be dismissed as an accident but could only be explained as an intentional act of a punitive deity.

Some clergy and laity viewed the catastrophe as a consequence of the sinfulness of the population, the increase in crime rate and race riots in Los Angeles. Others dismissed all religious explanations and accepted the earthquake as a seismic accident that carried no religious significance.

My own response to the questioners was based on the distinction I have drawn in this chapter between Elohim, the God of nature, and Adonai, the God of morality. I explained that there is no reason for religious people to quarrel with the descriptive analysis of the seismologists and geologists. There were no divine intentions or judgments in the earthquake. The laws of gravitation and plate tectonics are clearly not like moral laws that must be obeyed or else punishment will be visited on the violators of the law. In this regard the earthquake phenomenon is fault-free. Nature is not culpable.

Where was Divinity in the earthquake? Elohim was in

the dynamics of the earthquake, but not as a purposive agent executing an "act of God." Adonai was evident in the earthquake through the response of firemen, policemen, doctors, and neighbors who helped restore lives, calm the frightened, and rebuild the shattered lives of those around them. In their individual and collective behavior the community testifies to the reality of Adonai without denying the reality of Elohim. Left with the God of Elohim alone, we are pushed toward an amoral pantheism, a worship of nature. Without the idea of Elohim, we gravitate toward a position of denial.

Distinctions are in order. Elohim and Adonai are not the same but are ideally interdependent. The prophet Zechariah (14:9) spoke of that day when the names of Elohim and Adonai will be unified. The sons and daughters of the unified deity know both the powers of nature and the powers of human nature. They struggle to emulate that ideal of oneness in their own lives.

At services after the earthquake I submitted to the congregation a poem that summarized the religious implications of the earthquake.

ELOHIM-ADONAI

Blessed art Thou O Lord our God, King of the universe,
whose strength and might fill the world.

Elohim creates day and night,
light and darkness.
  Lion and lamb,
    bacteria and penicillin.
Gives power to the fowl above the earth,
To the great sea monsters below,
To every living creature that creeps on the earth.

And Elohim said,
   It is very good.
All existence is good in the eyes of
Elohim, the God of the first chapter of Genesis,
   Elohim who spoke to Job
   out of the whirlwind.

Who laid the cornerstones of earth?
Who shut up the sea with doors
When it broke forth and issued out of the womb?
Who caused it to rain on a land where no man is?
On the wilderness, wherein there is no man?

   Elohim the God of Omnipotence before whom
we recognize our own impotence,
   "Canst Thou bind the chain of the Pleiades
or loose the bands of Orion?"
Elohim the God of Omniscience before whom
   we recognize our ignorance,
"Do you know the ordinances of the heavens?
Can you number the clouds by wisdom?"
Elohim before whom we bow our heads
and bend our knees,
   the sovereign God whose power and reality we accept.

   But Elohim is not the whole of divinity.
Alongside Elohim is Adonai.
This is our affirmation of oneness.
Hear Israel, Adonai our Elohim is One.
Alongside Elohim the God of all that is stands
Adonai the Lord of all that ought to be.
Adonai revealed in the yearning of His human creation for
justice,
   for fairness,
   for peace,
   for harmony.

Adonai in the vision of a compassionate society.
Adonai in the transformation of chaos and violence and
   the void of the universe
    into order, sanity, and love.

Adonai in the mending of the universe,
   the repair of the world,
   the binding of bruises,
gathering up the fragmented sparks buried
in the husks of the world.

Adonai in the discovery of the self created in the image of
Adonai-Elohim, the Lord God, who breathed into our
nostrils and made us a living soul.

Elohim/Adonai,
Acceptance and transformation,
   the reality of what is, the reality of what ought to be,
   the reality yet to be.

CHAPTER EIGHT

In Search of Godliness

God is not a man that He should lie,
neither the son of man that He should repent:
hath He said and shall He not do it?
Or hath He spoken and shall He not make it good?

Numbers 23:19

Even with the distinctions between Elohim and Adonai, the same kind of questions persevere. Even if we did nothing, especially if we were blameless, why didn't Adonai intervene? Why did He not say no to the cancer, earthquake, or mass murderer?

The persistence of the question I trace to the conventional root assumption that God is most like a Person, and like a Person has His own designs. We may not fathom the purpose of the design but we know that some purpose lies behind His ways and that in God's eyes it is good. Particularly in the case of suffering, this deeply ingrained belief in God as a Person invites our ascription of some motivation to God. This mind-reading of the divine Person raises doubts of His goodness and intention.

The idea of God as a Person appears early in our spiritual biographies. In her Sunday class, Annie concentrated on her drawing. When her teacher asked what she was drawing, she replied casually, "I'm drawing a picture of God." Spotting a budding heretic, the teacher quickly intervened. "Annie, no one knows what God looks like." Annie replied, "But they will when I'm finished."

Annie's drawing appears naive, a circular portrait of a bearded sky God who looks down upon us. Nevertheless, it is retained in the mental picture of many adults and passed on from generation to generation. What is attractive about the drawing is its intimacy that promises accessibility to God. There is a family resemblance between God and us. It is true that religious philosophers have long warned against the fallacies of anthropomorphism that ascribe human characteristics to God and the projected anthropopathism that attributes human feelings to God. Still, the need to recognize and be recognized by God, the joy of familiarity with God, overrides the philosopher's critique. If I am like God, then God must in some sense be like me. God is no stranger. Rabbinic imagination ascribes human emotions to God, even inventing a prayer for God to Himself: "May it be My will that My compassion may overcome My anger and that it may prevail over My attribution of justice and judgment and that I may deal with My children according to the attribute of compassion and that I may not act towards these according to the strict line of justice" (Talmud Berachoth 7a). In rabbinic imagination, God is said to don His phylacteries, wrap Himself in the fringe of the prayer shawl, engage in Torah study, and cry for the loss of His temple.

There is, however, a critical flaw in the drawing. Once I conceive of God as a person like myself, He becomes open to criticism. The paradigm case in the Bible is that of Abraham confronting the sovereign God with righteous indignation: "Shall the judge of all the earth not do justly?" God as a moral person is drawn too close for comfort. If God is to retain His sovereignty, His vulnerability to criticism must be shielded.

Here enter the religious doctors who in defense of God insist on differentiating God from human beings. God hears, thinks, feels, and acts—but not as we hear, think, feel, and act. The theologians fall back on the prophet's defense: "For as the heavens are higher than the earth so are My ways higher than your ways and My thoughts than your thoughts" (Isaiah 55:9). To protect God, the theological defenders maintain that Annie's drawing must be discarded. God is not like us. God is different not only in degree but also in kind. If we call God all knowing, all powerful, all good, these cannot refer to the same kind of qualities we understand when speaking of qualities in humans. This amounts to declaring that God cannot be said to be moral in the manner that we are said to be moral.

That very moral distancing of God from ourselves raises deep resentments. We hear it in the outburst of the philosopher John Stuart Mill: "I will call no being good who is not what I mean when I apply the epithet to my fellow creatures, and if such a being can sentence me to hell, to hell I will go." To blunt Mill's assault, the original intimacy between God and man that is so compelling in Annie's picture must be redrawn. God is now portrayed as standing against man. In elevating God, the human being is now drawn increasingly subordinate to the will and acts of God. An alienating dualism has intruded in the original picture, splitting the divine and the human, "above" from "below." As a result, the questions about prayer, miracles, and revelation that I have dealt with are turned into forced either/or options. Prayer is either a unilateral response from God or a lonely human monologue; miracle is either God's intervention or human invention; revelation is either God's word cast down from above or a soliloquy from below.

We have been taught to think of God as a noun: it names something. To protect that noun from human moral criticism, the qualities that describe it cannot retain the meanings they have in everyday use. The qualities of God's love, justice, and compassion are not ours. The price for making the God-noun invulnerable to human judgment is, in effect, to free it from any and all moral qualifications. The noun stands detached from verbs, adverbs, adjectives. Consequently, the human-divine discourse of the dialogue is broken. I suggest another way to understand God that allows active human participation in the life of divinity.

From Noun to Verb

I propose a shift of focus, from noun to verb, from subject to predicate, from God as person to Godliness, in Hebrew Elohuth. Not the qualities of divinity but the divinity of the qualities is essential to belief. To illustrate this inversion, I turn to the liturgical life and specifically to the translation of benedictions. How are the blessings of the prayer book to be understood in accordance with the idea of Godliness? One of the first blessings we learn is the benediction over bread: "Blessed art thou O Lord our God King of the universe who brings forth bread from the earth." With the idea of Godliness our attention is directed not to the noun but to the activity that brings forth bread from the earth. What are the events that bring this bread to the table?

The benediction is a meditation on the transactions between nature and human beings. The transactions involve the givenness of the earth, water, sun, and seed (attributed to Elohim, God) and the preparations of the soil, the weeding and plowing, grinding, and baking (attributed to Adonai, the Lord that through human beings transforms nature). According to Rabbi Ben Zoma in the Talmud:

> What labors Adam had to carry out before he obtained
> bread to eat. He plowed, he sowed, he reaped, he bound
> with sheaves, he threshed and winnowed and selected the
> ears, he ground them and sifted the flour, he kneaded and
> baked till then at last he ate. Whereas when I get up I find
> all these things done for me. And how many labors Adam
> had to carry out before he had a garment to wear? He had

to shear, wash the wool, comb it, spin it and weave it, and then at last he obtained a garment to wear. Whereas when I get up I find all these things done for me. All kinds of craftsmen come early to the door of my house and I arise in the morning and find all these things before me.

Benedictions express praise of the unity of Elohim, the ground of nature, and Adonai, the source of transformation. Blessings acknowledge the cooperation of heaven and earth that hallows God's creation with the work of human hands. The intention of the benediction is inclusive: nature and human nature, the divine within the givenness and within the process of transforming it.

This reformulation counters the objections of critics such as the nineteenth-century philosopher Ludwig Feuerbach, who took religion to task for creating human alienation. He charged religion with draining the noble qualities from man to offer them up to God. As he saw it, religion offered praise to God by denying praise to man. Feuerbach's critique calls to mind the response of the farmer who at harvest time proudly showed the visiting rabbi the lush field of corn and wheat that he had labored to cultivate. The rabbi declared: "Give thanks to God my son. You and He are partners in this harvest." The farmer responded: "Rabbi, you should have seen this field when God was the sole owner." Prayers of gratitude, appreciation, and petition must include the efforts of humanity. There can be no jealousy between God and man. Human effort and intention to enrich and repair are not activities separate from God. They are the vital acts of Godliness.

The Gerunds of Godliness

I want to refocus the classic benedictions. Healing the sick, . . . clothing the naked, . . . releasing the bound, . . . raising up the fallen are the "divine activities" found not there or here, in me or within you, but in the relationship between our human and nonhuman environment. Godliness is in the activity of doing justly, healing the sick, raising the fallen, supporting the disadvantaged, uniting the real and ideal.

To believe in Godliness is to believe in the verbs and adverbs that refer to the activities of divinity. To behave in a Godly fashion is to realize in one's life the attributes of Godliness that are potential in all human and nonhuman energies. Atheism is not the disbelief in the reality and goodness of the noun but disbelief in the reality and goodness of the attributes. The question to be asked of those who seek God is not whether they believe in a noun that cannot be known but whether they believe in the gerunds of Godliness: healing the sick, feeding the hungry, supporting the fallen, pursuing peace, loving the neighbor. The imperatives of Godliness call the seeker to imitate the ways of Godliness.

The idea of Elohuth or Godliness that favors verbs over nouns has roots in the tradition. Abraham Joshua Heschel wrote: "We have no nouns by which to express His essence; we have only adverbs by which to indicate the ways in which He acts." For Heschel, a noun presupposes comprehension. Calling God by name means that we know Him in the manner that we know other noun names. But in the Bible, Moses' constant demand to know God's name is rejected. God is "I am what I am" or "I will be what I will be" (Exodus 3:14). God is not a static noun but a dynamic verb encompassing past, present, and future states of being. God is not a subject or an object. God is known only in relationship and only in situations that bear upon man.

The focus on the Godly attributes that make up Godliness instead of viewing God as an unknown subject noun possesses a venerable history. Both mystic and rationalistic Jewish theologies agree on the unknowability of God in itself whose essence cannot be named or pronounced or seen. For the mystics the infinite God is concealed and beyond the reach of our intellect. The rationalist Moses Maimonides agreed that God's essence is unknowable and that even His qualities may be grasped solely in terms of what they are not. Thus God's goodness, life, and power mean at most that God is not evil or lifeless or impotent. If we know anything about Divinity, it is not God the noun but God the verb, not God the inscrutable person but God's knowable qualities that may be emulated. What is it then to know God? The prophet explained that when the king "judged the cause of the poor and needy, then it was well with him. Was this not to know Me, saith the Lord?" (Jeremiah 22:16). Godliness is behaved. Godliness is believed through doing justice, in caring, in curing, in protecting. To behave in Godly fashion, is this not to know the divine? The twentieth-century thinker Franz Rosenzweig asserted, "Truth is a noun only for God; for us it is an adverb."

Is Godliness One?

No prayer is more embedded in Jewish consciousness than the one enunciating God's unity: "Hear O Israel the

Lord our God the Lord is One." In what sense is Godliness to be called One, since its qualities such as compassion, intelligence, and justice are many? The qualities of Godliness are not united by virtue of their residence in a single person. They are One by virtue of sharing a common purpose. The qualities of Godliness are interdependent. Intelligence, for example, without compassion, can hurt others. Compassion unqualified by intelligence can lead to folly. In this important sense, the qualities of divinity are correctives. They need each other. Justice without compassion can turn virtue into vice. Compassion without justice can lead to anarchy. The qualities of Godliness complement each other. To declare the Oneness of Godliness is to strive for harmony.

It is the idolater who worships single attributes as if they were the whole of Godliness. As the book of the Zohar proclaims: "Woe to the man who compares God with any single attribute of God." To unite and balance the attributes of Godliness in the self and in the world is the ideal to be achieved. In that day Godliness will be One and its name One.

Can There Be Godliness Without Human Beings?

Given the elevation of the status and responsibility of the human being, is Godliness dependent on the existence of human beings? Is there God or Godliness without humanity? The question may be answered by way of analogy. Can there be parents without children, teachers without students, or kings without subjects? Certainly without their correlative others they may exist as people, but not as parents, teachers, or kings. They may in the past have enjoyed the status of parents, teachers, and kings or may in the future function in those capacities. But without children, students, and subjects they cannot be said to own those roles.

Similarly, Elohim (God) without human beings exists, but not as Adonai (Lord). God as Elohim exists without people. Adonai as father, shepherd, teacher is inextricably bound to human beings. The relationship between divinity and humanity is expressed in the biblical verse in which God declares, "And I will take you to Me for a people and I will be to you a God and you shall know that I am the Lord your God who brings you out of the land of Egypt" (Exodus 6:7).

Pertinent to this argument is the mystical tradition of the Zohar, which insists that before creation, God was unknown and unknowable. After creation, He revealed himself and made known His attributes and His name, Adonai. Without man, God is not the Lord of the earth; without God, man is not fully human. The correlation of divinity and humanity is expressed in a major prayer recited during the Day of Atonement:

> For we are thy people and thou our God
> We are thy children and Thou our father
> We are thy servants and Thou our master
> We are thy congregants and Thou our portion
> We are thine inheritance and Thou our lot
> We are thy flock and Thou our shepherd
> We are thy vineyard and Thou our keeper
> We are thy work and Thou our creator
> We are thy faithful and Thou our beloved
> We are thy royal ones and Thou our lord
> We are thy subjects and Thou our king
> We are thy devoted people and Thou our exalted God.

CHAPTER NINE

The Place of Godliness in Transmitting the Memory of the Holocaust

And it shall be when thy child asketh of thee
in time to come saying "What is this?"
that thou shalt say . . .

Exodus 13:14

For many the huge obstacle in the path of traditional faith is the seeming impassiveness of God at the gates of Auschwitz. There the outstretched hand of the Lord of Exodus was shortened. God's immobility above appeared as a reflection of the passive bystanders below. No better He than those who closed the shutters of their windows and played with their dogs inside their homes; no different He from those who closed the borders of their country, turning back human refugees to the hands of gleeful executioners. A traumatized generation is left with terrifying memories. What should be done with them? Should they be transmitted to their children and, if so, how? In passing on holocaustal memories to our children do we place a stumbling block before the blind, pushing them inadvertently into a pit of despair? Not whether or not to remember but how to remember, not whether or not to have a past but what kind of past to hand down that is confounding.

The children sit in a darkened room during the annual commemoration of the Holocaust. Before them are the black and white pictures of pyramids of starved and charred bodies, the "excremental assault" on human innocence. They sit in silence. What do the children think? What do they feel? What will they remember? What will they learn about the nature of man and the nature of God?

I am torn with ambivalence. Surely though it happened before they were born, they must know. "Not to know what happened before you were born is to remain forever a child" (Cicero). Children should not be raised unknowing, in fatal ignorance.

To feign amnesia is to betray the victims of the past and the surviving generation. I want my children to know me, to understand my heightened sensitivity to the racial graffiti of the skinheads, the hateful rhetoric of David Duke

and Louis Farrakhan, the frightening megalomania of
Vladimir Zhirinovsky and Jean-Marie Le Pen. I want them
to understand my hard-earned paranoia and that of my
generation. To know me, to know us, is necessarily to
understand the Holocaust. The Holocaust remains the
dominant psychic reality of our lives. The gravity of the
statistics weighs heavy on us. One of three Jews in the
world decimated; two of every three Jews in Europe,
ninety percent of Eastern European Jewry, nine out of ten
rabbis, 1.5 million Jewish infants and children slaughtered
because of their Jewishness. How could it not affect us,
our moral sensibilities, our morale, our faith?

It is clear that the children must know it all. And yet I
wonder whether in transmitting the memory of the Holocaust I lay a stone upon their hearts. Do I plant in them the
seeds of cynicism, the type of schismatic thinking popular-
ized by Cynthia Ozick, who insists that "the whole world
wants us dead and has always wanted to wipe us out"?
Do I immortalize anti-Semitism and confirm the litany of
the Passover text "In every generation they rise against us
to destroy us"? Will they conclude from the Holocaust
that a primordial fissure within the human species splits
"them" from "us," they the children of Esau and we the
children of Jacob locked in eternal hatred? Do I inadvertently rob them of the possibility of normal and healthy
relationship with a non-Jewish world?

At such times Yudka comes to mind. Yudka is the character in Hayim Hazaz's short story The Sermon, who at a
kibbutz meeting rose before the assembly to declare, "I
want to state that I am opposed to Jewish history." The
normally diffident Yudka stammered out his fury: "I
would simply forbid teaching our children Jewish history.
Why the devil teach them about our ancestors' shame? I

would say to them 'Boys, from the day we were exiled from our land we have been a people without a history. Class dismissed. Go out and play football.'" I understand Yudka's frustration, his fear of spreading the contagion of despair to the children.

I confess that it is not only the children's morale that concerns me. The Holocaust is my own nightmare; it shakes the foundation of my faith. I meet men and women with memories deeper and more cruel than the numbers carved on their arms. Some break their silence and confide their darkest secrets. One such person, Dr. Walter Rothschild, a psychiatrist and friend, shared his memories of Kristallnacht, the long, dark night of shattered glass. That night, November 9, 1938—during which two hundred synagogues were destroyed, seven hundred Jewish businesses ransacked and burned, and twenty thousand Jewish men thrown into concentration camps—my friend's father, himself a physician in Frankfurt, was arrested by the Gestapo. He was dragged into a dark room and seated before a large table. On that table had been placed ten decapitated Jewish heads upon which the Nazis had placed ten skullcaps. One of the SS men taunted him, *"Jude, wir haben für Sie eine Minyan gesammelt!"* ("Jew, we have gathered a minyan for you!"; a minyan is the Jews' religious quorum). The cruel knowledgeability of the SS man deepens his hurt.

Shaking the Foundations of Faith

The Holocaust mocks my faith. For at the core of that faith is the conviction that God breathed into the nostrils of human beings an inviolable human soul, that God created the human being in His image and in His likeness. The taunting dissonance between that faith and the facts of the Holocaust disturbs my belief. The picture of a child hanged in the presence of parents in the concentration camp brings to mind a rabbinic commentary on the hanging of a criminal based on a verse in the book of Deuteronomy (21:23). A criminal sentenced to death and hanged must not remain overnight upon the tree because it is "a reproach unto God." Why a reproach unto God? The rabbinic answer is offered in the form of a parable. Once a noble king had a twin brother who violated the law and was hanged on a tree in the public square. People passing by the corpse of the king's twin took him to be the king and shouted, "Behold, the king is dead!" The king was humiliated. The parable is breathtaking. God and man are as it were twins. To deface the image of man is to blaspheme the Creator of that image. God is not raised by lowering the human image. Those who turn to God out of revulsion for man are like those who praise a parent while defaming his or her child. The psalmist declared, "Man abides in the shadow of the Almighty." A commentary explains that God is indeed like man's shadow. When the figure of man is lowered, the shadow contracts; when man is raised up, God is exalted.

Menachem Mendel of Vitebsk said, "All my life I have struggled in vain to know what man is. Now I know. Man is the language of God." That language has been soiled. Who can walk through the corridors of the Holocaust Museum filled with evidence of human bestiality, observe the rooms that document massive betrayal and collusion in evil, look at the piles of shoes, glasses, and hair and declare, without blushing, praise of the goodness of man made "but little lower than the angels"? Who before the memory of cremated children can declare the twinship of God and man? The theological crisis wrought by the Shoah is radical. Not whether God is dead but whether we are dead; not whether God exists but whether goodness is real or merely the invention of human conceit. Read the memoirs, examine the exhibits. The evidence of the Holocaust hardly confirms the theistic humanism of the Bible. On the contrary, walk the corridors and you hear the echoes that corroborate the cynicism and pessimism that range from Thrasymachus and Callicles down to Machiavelli, Hobbes, Nietzsche, and Sigmund Freud. Walking the halls of the museum, the last thing that comes to mind is the verse "And God saw that it was good." Rather it brings to mind the judgment of Freud, who concluded that people "viewed their neighbor in order to gratify their aggressiveness, to exploit his capacity for work without recompense, to use him sexually without his consent, to seize his possessions, to humiliate him, to cause him pain, to torture and to kill him."

"Ye are My witnesses, says the Lord." To this statement from the book of Isaiah the commentary adds, "If you are My witnesses then I am God. If you are not My witnesses then I am as it were not God." What witness do we have to give from history? What empirical facts as testimony to the character of human nature and of God? Preachments and quotations are not enough. Facts are needed. Empirical evidence of the existence of goodness on earth. Where was God while all this took place? Elohim was in Auschwitz. We can adduce morally neutral factors—economic, political, military—that can be traced to the impartial energy of Elohim. This amoral dimension of divinity we described in an earlier chapter. But where was Adonai in Auschwitz? Where was the power and mystique of Adonai within the hell of the Holocaust?

Testimony to Adonai

In addition to the record of Jewish self-sacrificing heroism on behalf of endangered fellow Jews, I direct attention to the tens of thousands of non-Jews, Christian believers and non-believers, young and old who came from every walk of life to risk their lives and those of their children and who saved Jews pursued and persecuted by the Nazis and their collaborators. Some of these rescuers live among us. I have met many of them and I have read validated accounts of their actions by Jewish survivors in every land in which the Nazis trod. I have looked at the faces of these ordinary human beings, made of flesh and blood like our own, who hid people of another faith and another tradition in their closets, attics, sewers, pigsties, holes in the ground. It is of paramount importance to know of the risks to life by these non-Jews who forged passports, falsified baptismal certificates, and organized underground safety and escape routes.

I call special attention to these non-Jewish rescuers because they transcended their religious and ethnic circles and leapt into the leprous circle of the condemned. They did not chant the liturgy or recite the catechism of those they protected with their lives. They are heroes from the other side. In an era of so much polarization between "them" and "us," these heroes from the other side help dispel the dangerous stereotypes that paint the other side with a black brush.

In the early 60s when I served as a rabbi in Oakland, California, I received a call from a man who identified himself as Jacob Gilat, a nuclear chemist from Israel studying at the University of California in Berkeley, who said he must see me. He said he had a story that was important for me to hear. I did not know then how important that call would turn out to be, how much it would affect my understanding of the Holocaust, how it would help me to transmit memory to my children, how it would help strengthen my faith. Briefly put, Jacob Gilat during the Holocaust was a child of ten, his brother Shalom a child of seven, and his brother David aged five. They were all left by their parents (the Gutgelts) in the care of their Aunt Hannah in the Warsaw ghetto. A former Polish farmer and later a small businessman, Alex Roslan, saw Jewish children lying dead in the streets of the Warsaw ghetto: corpses of toddlers, teenagers, their bodies covered with swarming flies. He could not bear the sight of this callousness and cruelty. Roslan smuggled Jacob and his brothers out of the ghetto and hid them in his home with the grudging consent of his wife, Mila, who was worried about the fate of their own two young children, Yurek and Mary.

To hide a Jew in Poland, to offer a Jew food, drink, or shelter was a capital crime. To hide a Jew in Poland was to risk one's life and the life of one's family. All around there were the Nazi predators, Polish informants, the *schmalzowniki*, who would receive a quart of brandy, four pounds of sugar, and a carton of cigarettes for turning in Jews. In that environment two thousand five hundred Christian Poles were executed for helping Jews.

Jacob Gilat and his brother Shalom came down with scarlet fever, which infected Alex's own son, Yurek. Yurek was sent to the Warsaw hospital for treatment. Yurek, then ten years of age, took notes on what the doctors and nurses did to cure him. He took only half of the medicine given him, hid the rest, and then gave it to his parents to give to his Jewish "brothers" at home. It was regrettably not of great help. The Jewish boys needed to be admitted to the Warsaw hospital. Dr. Masurik, a surgeon, needed 100 zlotys to bribe members of the staff so that the Jewish children could be admitted and administered to at the hospital. To raise the money Alex Roslan sold his three-room apartment and moved to a one-room apartment. How did he smuggle a Jewish child into the hospital? With ingenuity, subterfuge, and courage. Shalom was brought to the hospital in a hollowed-out sofa, purportedly delivered as furniture for the waiting room of Dr. Masurik. Shalom died on the operating table, was brought home and buried in the Roslans' cellar. Alex Roslan would not surrender. For years he moved from home to home, built false walls in his cupboards, and got the German police drunk when they came to investigate rumors that he was sheltering Jews.

I remember my first strained encounter with Alex Roslan. I am a child of Polish Jewish parents whose memories were filled with Polish anti-Semitism, name calling, beatings, and pogroms. Here was Alex Roslan, a Polish Gentile. Beside me stood Jacob Gilat, his life and death witness. Alex Roslan is my friend, a friend of my people. The testimony of his behavior and stance was a moment of transformation in my own life.

Shortly thereafter I met a German, Hermann Graebe, who was a railroad engineer in the Ukraine in the city of Rovnow. Graebe witnessed the slaughter of hundreds of Jewish men and women who were then dumped into a pit. Hermann Graebe requisitioned hundreds of Jews, placed them into work details, and established an underground escape route around a fictitious branch office in Poltawa in the Ukraine. During three years of his daring work, Graebe spent over $200,000 of his own money for food, clothing, and identification papers for Jews. He also testified against the Nazis at the Nuremberg trials. When he died his family asked me to officiate at his church funeral along with his Lutheran minister. After the services I met with dozens of those he rescued. They were in the pews mourning the death of Graebe, the Moses of Rovnow, who had saved 348 Jews.

Where was Adonai in the Holocaust? Adonai was in Niuvelande, a Dutch village in which seven hundred residents rescued five hundred Jews, including one hundred Jewish children. The entire population of Niuvelande acted as rescuers. Every single household took one Jewish family or at least one Jew into their home. No one feared being informed upon by his neighbor because everyone was implicated in the crime of concealing a Jew. Adonai was among the simple folk, the house painters, bakers, postmen, who met frightened children at the trains and gave them food, shelter, and love in their own homes.

Adonai was in Le Chambon-sur-Lignon, whose citizens hid and protected five thousand Jews under the inspired leadership of Pastor André Trocmé.

Adonai was in the rat-infested sewers of Lvov, where Polish sewer workers hid seventeen Jews for fourteen months.

Adonai was in Bulgaria, an Axis ally of Germany. When deportation orders were given to expel all Jews from Bulgaria, Dmiter Peshov of the Sobranie (the Bulgarian parliament) and Bishop Kiril of the Bulgarian Orthodox Church sought to defy that order. Bishop Kiril wired King Boris III, demanded that he resist the Nazi order, and informed him that his soul stood in mortal danger if he acquiesced to the Nazis. The bishop told King Boris that he and his parishioners would lay their bodies on the railway track before they would allow deportation. The deportation order led to such an outcry from the Bulgarian people that the order was rescinded and the Jews taken into custody were released. March 10th came to be known in Bulgaria as a miraculous day for the Jewish people. Ninety percent of Bulgarian Jews were saved from death.

In remembering the Holocaust, Jewish and non-Jewish children should know that in similar fashion three thousand Jews in Finland were saved. Finnish intelligence penetrated Himmler's apartment in Helsinki and photographed the contents of his portfolio, which contained detailed plans for the "final solution" of the Finnish Jews. Despite the pressure from Himmler to deport the Jews, the Finnish cabinet would not surrender "our Jews." Finnish Foreign Minister Witting explained, "Finland is a decent nation. We would rather perish together with the Jews than give them up."

Adonai was with the Italian troops stationed in the southwestern half of Croatia; with General Roatta and General Robotti, who refused to turn over the thousands of Jews who fled to the Italian zone; with Italian authorities, diplomats, and generals who would not yield to the repeated pressures of the Nazis to transport Jews into the hands of the murderers. Wherever the Italian army was the occupying force—in Yugoslavia, Greece, southern France, Albania—it protected the Jews from their own German Axis allies. The Fascists controlled Croatia and when the fanatic Utashe Party openly proclaimed the liquidation of all Jews as its first priority, Jews fled to the safety of the Italian controlled zone.

On Black Sabbath a raid was organized by the Nazis who occupied Italy. The Germans expected to capture eight thousand Jews. They were frustrated by the Italian citizenry. Seven thousand Jews found hiding places among sympathetic Italians. Citizens of Italy rescued the lives of forty thousand Jews, eighty-five percent of the Jewish population.

In every land occupied by the Nazis there were persons who would not feign blindness and muteness. Even in Berlin eleven hundred Jews survived the Nazi scourge by finding refuge among decent Germans throughout the war.

In remembering the cruelty and barbarity of the Holocaust, we must not forget the moral heroes of conscience. In an era of the anti-hero, the heroes of conscience must be exalted. Aristedes De Sousa Mendes was the Portuguese Consul General in Bordeaux, France during the war. Refugees were fleeing France, thousands desperately seeking visas to escape from the clutches of the Nazis. The Portuguese government banned the passage of refugees into their country. Mendes was approached by Rabbi Chayim Kreiger, who explained the fear, panic, and imminent doom of the Jewish refugees. Mendes sat up with the rabbi all night without food or sleep and helped stamp thousands of passports with Portuguese visas. He did not eat or sleep and told his staff, "My government has denied application for visas for any refugees but I cannot allow these people to die. We are going to issue a visa to anyone who asks for it regardless of whether or not he can pay." Mendes was recalled for disobeying instructions. Upon his return to Lisbon, the Portuguese government, fuming at Mendes's insubordination, appointed a committee to investigate his action. He was summarily dismissed from the Foreign Ministry with all retirement and severance benefits suspended. Mendes, with a family of twelve children and with no other means at his disposal, was forced to sell his ancient family estate in Cabanas De Virato. He died in 1954 forgotten, heartbroken, impoverished. Mendes was a Catholic. Asked why he acted as he did, he replied, "If thousands of Jews can suffer because of one Catholic [i.e., Hitler], surely it is permitted for one Catholic to suffer for so many Jews. I could not act otherwise. I accept everything that has befallen me with love." Mendes was responsible for saving ten thousand Jews.

Sempo Sugihara was the Japanese Consul General in Kovna, Lithuania. In the summer of 1940 he issued transit visas to Jews imperiled, people who came to him with death staring them in the eyes. Sugihara saw their tears and fear. He said, "Whatever punishment may be imposed upon me, I know that I should follow my conscience." The Japanese Foreign Ministry ordered him to cease and desist from issuing visas. Sugihara granted thousands of transit visas to Polish Jews. With the help of one of the yeshiva students, he worked feverishly for twelve consecutive days until his departure from Kovna. At the end of the war, he returned to Japan and was summarily dismissed due to his "neglect of instructions." He died unknown and unheralded. He saved the lives of three thousand five hundred Jews.

Should Jewish and non-Jewish children not be taught, along with the unspeakable atrocities of the Holocaust, the incredible exploits of a police commandant at St. Gallen, Switzerland named Paul Grüninger? His assignment was to prevent Jewish refugees from illegally entering Switzerland from Germany. One day he said to his wife, "I cannot send these people back." He predated the official police seals on the refugees' passports to make it appear that they had entered the country before the ban. The SS discovered his crime. The Swiss authorities put him on trial, dismissed him from the police force, and found him guilty of *amstpflichtverletzung*, malfeasance, betrayal, insubordination. In February 1985, the St. Gallen Regional Council offered a motion to grant him a full posthumous rehabilitation. That motion was defeated. Grüninger saved three thousand Jewish refugees.

How Many Were There?

Holocaust scholars now estimate that there were between fifty thousand and five hundred thousand Christian rescuers. Whatever the number, there were too few. Sadly there are always too few moral heroes in history. Should quantity be the measure of moral quality? The Jewish religious tradition maintains that for the sake of thirty-six righteous persons the world was saved, and that for the sake of ten righteous persons Sodom and Gomorrah would not have been destroyed.

There are some who nevertheless are less than enthusiastic about the recognition of rescuers. They fear that these accounts of moral heroism may somehow appear to mitigate the tragic severity of the Holocaust. I answer that there are no heroes without villains. There are no Graebes without Mengeles, no Oskar Schindlers without Amon Goeths. Besides which the moral question is whether the bones of the rescuers should be interred with the predators. Abraham at Sodom drew near to God, insisting that God would not "sweep away the righteous with the wicked" (Genesis 18:23).

The moral art in transmitting the memory of the Holocaust requires that the evidence of goodness not be buried
in anonymity or lost in a footnote or damned with faint
praise. Consider the *Encyclopedia Judaica*'s description of
the Anne Frank story, in which a family of eight were kept
in hiding for over two years. The entry includes a sparse
seven words regarding those who hid them: "They were
kept alive by friendly Gentiles." Who were they? What
happened to them after they were betrayed by informers
and some sent to Amersfort concentration camp? What are
their names? How ironic that our children and we ourselves know the names of Klaus Barbie, Goebbels, Goer-
ing, Eichmann, Himmler, and Hitler but not the names of
those who risked their lives to hide and protect the Frank
family. Are not the names of Victor Kugler and Jan Klein-
man and Miep Giess and Elizabeth Van Vosquijl to be
remembered in remembering the Holocaust?

When the rescuers are asked "Why did you risk all
this?" they typically respond "What else could I do?
What would you do?" The question places a mirror to
my soul. Would I open the door? Would I hide this pursued pregnant woman? Would I take care of her needs?
When rations during the war were so meager would I
risk getting extra food without raising suspicion? Would
I take an infant into my home whose cries might reveal
our hiding place? What would I do with their refuse or
with their bodies after their death? Stefa Krakowska, a
Polish peasant, hid fourteen persons in her home, rang-
ing from age three to age sixty, in a home in which a simple pail served as the toilet. When an older Jewish
woman fell sick and knew herself to be dying, she turned
to Stefa. "My God, my dead body may bring disaster to
you. What will you do with my body?" She feared for the

others' safety. She died. At night, secretly and in stages they buried her dismembered body in Stefa's garden. "There are times," the philosopher Frederick Woodbridge wrote, "when a person ought to be more afraid of living than of dying."

Why is this phenomenon of altruism so important when we tell the children the tragic history of the Holocaust? Will it alleviate the pain or reverse the outcome? To apply the words of the Israeli poet Dan Pagin, we cannot "turn the scream back into the throat or the gold teeth back into the gums or the yellow star back into the sky." But with this unheralded evidence of moral heroism brought to light we can correct the distortion of history that no one cared, that no church helped, that there was no conspiracy of goodness in the lands where the Nazi shadow fell. That canard not only distorts the past but cripples the future because it is used by some to insist that there were no allies, are no allies, and never will be any allies to call upon. That dismissal of the evidence of rescue, however small, helps twist history into a metaphysical fatalism that ordains anti-Semitism as an eternal recurrence. Beneath the cry "Never again!" is whispered a deeper pessimistic verdict on all Jewish history: "Ever again." Salo Baron, the eminent Jewish historian, struggled against this "lachrymose conception of history." The events of the Holocaust are sad enough not to use it to forecast the Jewish future. It has led many to retreat to an insular enclave and to adopt an isolationism of despair. The bending of history into a bifurcating metaphysics that violates the memory of the good destroys the hope for the possibilities of the future. We do no honor to the victims and martyrs of the Holocaust by transmogrifying its incomparable tragedy into a polarizing philosophy. Paralyzing pessimism is not the lesson to be learned from the art of memory. "If all you have is a hammer the world is filled with nails."

What Is Man?

Witness to the phenomenon of altruism in the hell of the Holocaust helps correct the distorted metapsychology of those like the philosopher George Santayana, who was convinced that generous impulses were occasional or self-deceptive hypocrisies. "Strain the situation, however, dig a little beneath the surface, and you will find a ferocious, persistent, profoundly selfish man." The playwright Tennessee Williams reflects this morbid characterization of human nature when he declares that "the only honest man is an unabashed egoist . . . the specific ends of life are sex and money, so the human comedy is an outrageous medley of lechery, alcoholism, homosexuality, blasphemy, greed, brutality, hatred, obscenity."

I have often wondered what these writers would make of the altruism of the Holocaust rescuers. How would they dismiss the nobility of Anne Borkowskaw, the Mother Superior of a Benedictine convent outside the ghetto of Vilna, who with six Catholic sisters risked her life by hiding Jewish leaders like Abba Kovner, Abraham Sutzgever, Edith Borok, and Ari Wilner in nuns' habits? When in the winter of 1941 the Jewish Fighters Organization was formed in the Vilna ghetto, the Mother Superior, assisted by other nuns, roamed the countryside in search of knives, daggers, pistols, and grenades to smuggle in to the Jewish fighters. The same hands that fingered rosary beads became expert in handling explosives. She said to Abba

Kovner, a Marxist and avowed atheist, "I wish to come to the ghetto to fight by your side, to die if necessary. You are closer to God than I." What would Santayana or Williams say of the tens of thousands of rescuers whose situation was quite strained and whose generous impulses often cost them their security, their safety—and their lives?

The importance of identifying and recounting and elevating the Christian rescuers of Jews has profound implications for the faith, morals and morale of our children. In a post-Holocaust world we need to be reminded that we are human beings. The witnessed narratives of goodness help restore a more balanced portrait of human nature. Primo Levi's encounter with Lorenzo, the non-Jewish Italian worker who brought him a piece of bread and the remainder of his ration every day for six months in Auschwitz, produced in Levi a renewed faith. "I believe it was really due to Lorenzo that I am alive today. Not so much because of his material aid as for his having constantly reminded me by his presence, by his natural and plain manner of being good, that there still exists a just world outside our own, something and someone still pure and whole, not corrupt and savage. Thanks to Lorenzo I managed not to forget that I myself was a man." (*Survival in Auschwitz*)

In recalling the Holocaust our children must be taught not to forget that there were human beings and that they are human beings. They must be reminded that there was and always are alternatives to passive complicity with cruel powers; that there were men and women of flesh and blood like their own who "turned themselves into hiding places from the wind and shelters from the tempests" (Isaiah 32:2). They must be taught that goodness did not always come in grandiose measure, but in a boiled

potato, a mashed strawberry, a piece of bread. Goodness
came in individual and collective gestures such as those
described in Terrence Des Pres' *The Survivors*. He tells of
the frequent and lengthy lineups in the camps where faint-
ing from exhaustion led to the gas chambers. In many
instances the inmates leaned hard against one another to
prevent their weaker peers from collapsing.

Should children in remembering the Holocaust years
know only the curses of the killers of the dream and not
the blessings of the protectors? Memory must keep an eye
on the future. If it is blind to its moral potential, memory
leaves in its wake a dark and paralyzing depression. It is
not necessary to falsify the past in order to sustain the
morale of our children. It *is* necessary to unearth the reality of goodness so that children can retain "the basic trust"
that psychoanalyst Erik Erikson maintained is essential for
their vitality. "Basic trust" is not Pollyanna faith but in
Erikson's words retains "a favorable ratio of basic trust
over basic distrust." In religious language "basic trust" is
an essential attribute of *emunah*, or faith.

We have in the earlier chapters spoken of the ambiguity
of evil, moral conscience, and Godliness. In the phenomenon of altruism in the midst of holocaustal terror
those subjects are powerfully illustrated, as they are in the
film *Schindler's List*. If that film has become the defining
symbol of the Holocaust, it is, I believe, not because of its
artistry alone, but because it enables the viewer to enter
the dark cavern without feeling that there is no exit. "How
far that little candle throws its beam." Memory of the
Holocaust is a sacred act that elicits a double mandate: to
expose the depth of evil and to raise goodness from the
dust of amnesia.

It is told of the Baal Shem Tov, the master of the good

name, that he dreamt one night that an evil heart stood before him. All the darkest forces in the universe were concentrated in it. The master clenched his fist and pounded and pummeled the evil heart, meaning to kill it. At that moment, he heard the cry of an infant emitted from that heart of evil. The Baal Shem Tov stopped in wonder. How could the voice of innocence be locked in such a hellish receptacle?

CHAPTER TEN

Why Should I Be Religious?

All my life I have
struggled in vain
to know what man is.
Now I know that man
is the language of God.

Menachem Mendel of Vitebsk

David, whom we met in the introductory chapter, identifies himself as a spiritual person who cannot believe. "Why," he asks, "should I be religious?" I have sought to remove the obstacles to his faith by acknowledging some of the shortcomings of conventional theology and by offering alternative interpretations of beliefs within the tradition. David remains ambivalent. He is drawn to many of the options I have proposed, but he has reservations about the authenticity of these new interpretations.

Paradoxically, the only religious notions he considers authentic are those he cannot believe; the only ones he can believe are those he thinks to be inauthentic. When David asks why he should be religious, he has in mind "the old-time religion" he vaguely remembers but disbelieves. As far as religion is concerned, David possesses a monolithic mindset. For him religious belief should be immune from change or reinterpretation. Ironically, for him, to be "religious" is to accept the very notions of religion he cannot believe. He is precommitted to a sameness of religious belief to which he cannot subscribe. David's mindset makes it easy for him to reject being religious. His view of Judaism forecloses all options to refine or reinterpret religious beliefs and practices. Consciously or not he has created a ready excuse for apostasy. David has chosen not to choose. According to his either/or approach, choosing other options to the notions he has picked up in his youth is to accept heresies.

If David is ever to be convinced to believe he must be exposed to the pluralistic character of Jewish faith. He must come to know the authenticity of change and the multiplicity of interpretations within the tradition. The Torah is one, but the commentaries are many and often contradictory. The rationalistic God idea of Maimonides is quite other than the existentialist God idea of Judah Halevi or the mystic God idea of Isaac Luria or the naturalistic God idea of Mordecai M. Kaplan. Babylonian and Palestinian Jewry did not interpret the law the same way nor did Ashkenazic and Sephardic Jewry possess the same liturgy.

The Talmud itself records conflicting rulings and interpretations of the sages. They were quite aware that situations change, that what was once permitted may later be prohibited and that what was once proscribed may later be allowed. The rabbinic schools of Hillel and Shammai argued, debated, and disagreed with each other on major issues, but the opinions of both schools were recorded, because as one commentator explained, there are times when one reason will be valid and other times when a contrary reason will be valid. Both schools were considered as reflecting the word of God.

The prophet Jeremiah compared God's word to "a hammer that breaks a rock in many pieces" (Jeremiah 23:29). The rabbis commented that, "As the hammer causes numerous sparks to flash forth, so a scriptural verse engenders many interpretations" (Talmud Sanhedrin 34a).

In a rabbinic parable God is said to appear to the children of Israel at Mount Sinai as a mirror. A thousand faces may look at it and it reflects each of them. The mirror is one, the reflections are many, and all of them are the images of divinity. Pluralism then is no alien notion but is intrinsic to the character of Judaism. Without appreciation of the pluralistic character of Judaism, David will remain ensconced in his disbelief.

Observance

When he speaks of being religious David means more than ideas and beliefs. He has in mind ritual observances. In this he is correct because Judaism places considerable emphasis on concrete practices and observances. But here again David's experience in the world of ritual is far from enthusiastic and here again his conventional religious experience confirms his dissatisfaction. He reports his boredom with the repetitiveness of prayers and the routinization of rituals. He recalls being taught "the rite thing" but nothing of its spiritual meaning. He is not alone or peculiarly modern in his complaints. In the sixth century the prophet Isaiah castigated the people in God's name because they have "approached Me with a mouth and honored Me with its lips, but has kept its heart far from Me and its worship of Me has been a commandment of man, learned by rote" (Isaiah 29:13).

The response to David should be obvious. Rituals should be taught with a rationale of heart and mind. But many conventional religious educators disagree. People, they maintain, believe what they do more than they do what they believe. They feel what they do more than they do what they feel. They know what they do more than they do what they know. Believing is not doing. Feeling is not doing. Knowing is not doing. Only doing is doing. Belonging, feeling, knowing therefore follow upon doing. "We shall do" precedes "we shall hear."

There is a pragmatic wisdom in orthopraxy, straight practice. Its adherents argue that rationale endangers the continuity of observance. They cite King Solomon's transgressions as evidence of the precariousness of offering rationale. The king claimed to know the reasons that the Bible forbids the kings of Israel to multiply wives and acquire horses (Deuteronomy 17:16–17). Therefore, he multiplied wives and acquired horses bolstered by his conviction that knowing the reasons for the prohibitions he would not be enticed. But Solomon stumbled and fell. Such an episode gave rise to the rabbinic dictum that to observe the law because God commanded it is superior to observing the law on the basis of given reasons (Talmud Kiddushin 31a). Rationale then is said to produce a shaky foundation for observance. Far surer is practice that is based on obedience to God's command.

But David is not prepared to accept the commander-soldier model either theologically or morally. The logic of orthopraxy does not persuade those who insist that believing and knowing and feeling should be prior to behaving. I myself do not believe that offering rationale for ritual will jeopardize its practice. Should one rationale fail, others will take its place. Jewish history testifies to the capacity of the people and its leaders to uncover layers of meaning that buttress the ritual act. The discovery of rationale enhances and enlivens the ritual act. The multiplicity of Passover Seder texts after the Holocaust and the establishment of the State of Israel illustrate how new narratives may enlarge the relevance and rationale of the freedom motif and increase the motivation to observe.

The Role of Ritual at Home

Separating rationale from ritual or reason from emotion impoverishes both religious belief and religious observance. There is a wholeness in being religious that abhors compartmentalization. "To have religion," Mordecai Kaplan wrote, "a people must have other things besides religion." In Judaism those other things include attachment to the family, which is the vital vehicle through which values are transmitted and rituals exercised. Rituals celebrated within the ambiance of the home and the family are qualitatively different from those observed alone or in the sanctuary. In conversations with couples contemplating intermarriage the memories of the family Passover Seder or the family's Christmas tree decorations loom large in their respective consideration of conversion.

Fidelity to a particular faith is closely related to the nostalgia for the family's ways of celebration. Memories of melodies sung, stories told, aphorisms repeated, and foods shared are not formally included in being religious, but they assume an existential importance alongside theological creed and ritual deed.

The historian Burkhardt councils, "We are instructed by words and educated by our eyes." What has David seen at home and in the family? If he has seen nothing or if the wine was sanctified lovelessly and the bread was broken in anger, the loftiest theology will sour. There are limits beyond which the noblest philosophical and moral argumentation cannot reach. Those who, like David, missed the warmth and compassion of the family around the Sabbath table must create their own ancestry, their own Sabbath, and their own memories for their children.

Rites of Passage

The importance of rituals in our lives is especially felt in events such as birth or death when our emotions over-

whelm us and call for some sacred container. I recall offi-
ciating at the funeral of a professor's father and later
when we were alone being earnestly asked by the grieving son, "How can I mourn?" What was this secularly
sophisticated man asking? He sought a distinctive way
to hallow his loss in a manner that connected him and
his father with a larger universe. He sought to mourn his
father among the mourners of his people and within the
sacred liturgy of his ancestry. He wanted to raise his private grief and give it cosmic significance. He wanted to
invest it with a meaning that transcends his private loss.
Here ritual pays attention to the inchoate feelings of
human beings that call for a rooted connection between
the ache and emptiness of the present, the reverence for
the past, and the promise of the future. The rituals of
mourning surround the grieving emotions in a sheath of
meaning.

A similar need is sensed by parents of the newly born
child. How shall we celebrate the birth of our child? How
shall we channel our feelings, lift the event above the
ordinary, invest its significance beyond the biological,
hallow the wonder? What name are we to give, with
whom are we to celebrate, and where? Ritual solicits us
to not take things for granted. It urges us to observe and
to respect (respect from the Latin respicere, "to look
back").

There is more wisdom and ethics in ritual than is
dreamed of. Keeping David's searching questions in mind,
I turn to a discussion of personal rites of passage to illustrate how rituals and their rationale transmit the ethos and
mythos of a people.

Passages and the Circles of Identity

Martin Buber writes, "The extended lines of relations meet in the eternal Thou." Buber's insight is pertinent to our discussion of the role of the rites of passage in which identities and relationships converge. Taken whole, the rites of passage from birth to death trace a path of spiritual growth that corresponds to the search of the self for Godliness. Accompanying each stage of passage is a body of traditional interpretations that describe the route of the self and its place within the circles of its environment: family, community, humanity. The relationships celebrated in the rites of passage meet in the orbit of Godliness. If we draw a scheme of the network of relationships and identities that accompany the rites of passage they form a circle of circles within which Godliness reigns.

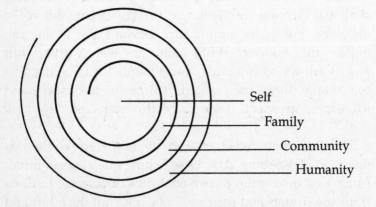

All the circles of Godliness are open. The self is drawn not as a completed entity but as a central referent in all the circles of relationship. Whatever voices are heard, visions seen or texts read are filtered through the self.

Godliness hovers over the face of relationship and cannot be reached by skipping over the human relationship. There is no shortcut to Godliness. Godliness is not an enclosed, separate entity. It is not a disembodied object to be sought and found. Godliness is not a circle like those of self, family, community, or humanity. Godliness is where the qualities of relationships meet.

Marriage

One of the earliest biblical observations declares, "It is not good for the human being to be alone" (Genesis 2:18). In the Garden of Eden, Adam had no need to labor with the sweat of his brow or to till the soil, clearing it of thorns and thistles. No enmity existed between him and the beasts of the forest. Adam lacked nothing except an other. Not any other; not the other of cattle or the fowl of the air or the beasts of the field (Genesis 2:20), but only an other to whom Adam could say "thou." He sought another like himself, bone of his bone, flesh of his flesh, and spirit of his spirit. It is only after Adam finds her, names her "woman" (*ishah*) that he himself is first called "man" (*ish*). It is through the human other that Adam discovers the dignity of his self.

As in every passage from one circle of identity to another, there is in marriage a felt experience of separation and attachment. "Therefore a man shall leave his father and his mother and cling to his wife so that they become as one flesh" (Genesis 2:24). The newly formed identity of husband and wife necessitates a break with an older identity. Both son and daughter are to leave their parents to shape their separate identities. The husband is not to be the wife's father nor the wife the husband's mother.

The rites of marriage demonstrate the transition of identities and loyalties. The syntax of relationship is transformed from "I," "me," and "mine" to "we," "us," and "ours." The merger, however, does not blur the individual integrity of each. Absorption of the self in another removes the ground of genuine dialogue. Menachem Mendel of Kotzk condensed this wisdom of the self in a subtle aphorism: "If I am I because I am I, and you are you because you are you, then I am I and you are you. But if I am I because you are you, and you are you because I am I, then I am not I and you are not you."

From the biblical account of the creation of Eve, elaborate myths spring to life. One such legend is based on the biblical text: "In the image of God created He him; male and female created He them" (Genesis 1:27). Rabbinic imagination portrays the first human being, Adam, as androgynous, possessing male and female characteristics within one undifferentiated self. The androgynous is self-sufficient. All genders are within it.

Still, Adam felt alienated. Seeing Adam's loneliness, the Lord God split the bisexual facade, creating male and female parts. The popular idiom "my better half" derives from this legend of separation that initiates the search of reunion. Of all animals, it is the human being alone who turns face-to-face in sexual intercourse. The solitary self is incomplete; it yearns for wholeness. Love tears asunder the embrace of the self. Love requires another who is not the extension of one's own self, an appendage of one's ego, a vessel into which one may pour one's own ambitions, fears, fantasies, angers. The separation symbolized by the splitting of the primordial facade prefigures the basic need for separateness in togetherness.

Marriage is a paradigm for human and divine coexistence. Within the tradition, love and marriage are major metaphors of spiritual relationships. The sages taught that when two love each other with all their heart, soul, and might, there God resides. If you would know God, love.

At the conclusion of the wedding ceremony, the bridegroom breaks a glass, an odd gesture at a ceremony whose benedictions are God's creation of mirth and exultation, pleasure and delight. Indeed, the blessing of God for creating happiness is recited only at the wedding and at no other rite of passage. Only at the celebration of union is the creation of joy blessed. What does breaking a glass have to do with union? The shattering of the glass suggests the unique version of cosmic creation as conceived by the sixteenth-century mystic Isaac Luria. For Luria, creation was not a consequence of God's expansiveness but a result of God's deliberate self-contraction.

In order to grant human beings space to exercise free will, God of His own withdrew into Himself. God's separation from the world is indispensable for an uncoerced relationship between man and God. But, the myth continues, a universe without God could not sustain itself. God therefore sent out a light of splendor to warm and enlighten the world. The world vessel, however, could not contain the fire of God. The vessel cracked and the sparks of divinity were scattered. The sparks remain in the dark crevices of the universe, waiting to be redeemed from captivity by the descendants of Adam and Eve.

The glass shattered by the groom representing the couple signifies the fragmented world, the brokenness of the human condition. The bride and groom who share the gift of love offer to use its blessings to release the sparks from the bondage of darkness. They pledge to use their talent for compassion and righteousness to make whole that which is divided and bind the wounds of humanity. The circle of marriage is inclusive.

A wedding ritual of some two millennia instructs the bride and groom each to hold a cup of wine and pour a portion of their wine into an empty cup. The empty cup represents the vessel of the world devoid of love. The mixing of the wine dramatizes the mingling of their lives, the strength gained in each other.

They have become as one, a conversion without loss of identity. "Where you go, I will go. Where you lodge, I will lodge. Your people shall be my people, your God, my God. Where you die, I will die and there I will be buried. Thus and more may the Lord do to me, if anything but death parts me from you" (Ruth 1:16).

Birth and Covenant

The biblical verse that follows the report of the expulsion of Adam and Eve from the Garden of Eden after eating from the prohibited tree of knowledge states: "And the man knew Eve his wife and she conceived and bore Cain and said 'I have gotten a man with the help of the Lord'" (Genesis 4:1). Kept away from the tree of life and denied immortality, Adam and Eve give birth to a child, their flesh-and-blood bond with the future. They know that after their death they will be present in the child. The first imperative of the first human beings is to multiply and fructify and fill the earth. Bearing a child carries with it cosmic significance. God "created the world not in vain. He formed it to be inhabited" (Isaiah 45:18).

Who is this newborn and into what world is the child cast? In existential dread, the philosopher Blaise Pascal cried out: "Cast into the immensity of spaces of which I am ignorant and which know me not, I am frightened." In the Jewish tradition the child is neither ignored nor ignorant. In rabbinic imagination the unborn soul is provided with angels who teach it the entire Torah. Shown heaven and earth, the consequences of good and bad behavior, the soul pleads with God not to enter the world. "I am well pleased with the world in which I have been living since the day on which Thou didst call me unto being. Why dost Thou now desire to have me enter this impure sperm, I who am holy and pure and part of Thy glory?" God consoles the soul: "The world which I shall cause thee to enter is better than the world in which thou hast lived hitherto and when I created thee, it was only for this purpose" (*Legends of the Jews*, Louis Ginsberg). The child enters the world pure of body and of spirit, uncontaminated by any stigma of original sin.

Before birth, a legend declares, the angel strikes the baby on the lip (which is popularly said to explain the indentation on our upper lip). With that blow, the child forgets all he or she has learned from the time that the soul was instructed. The child is born ignorant, but not as a clean slate. There is in the memory of the newborn soul a latent wisdom that can be revealed only through living. The myth instructs us that not knowledge but the struggle to learn is the end. At the covenant rite, the family pledges to lead the child into the ideals of the faith: "the study of Torah, the nuptial canopy and the practice of good deeds."

When the child is brought into the room where the

covenant ritual is to take place, the adults rise as a gesture of respect for a human being and recite, "Blessed be the one who arrives." A rabbinic statement expresses the spiritual humanism implicit in the act of standing. "Wherever you see the footprints of human beings, God stands before you. Wherever a human being walks abroad, he is preceded by a company of angels who call out, 'Make way for the image of God'" (Deuteronomy Rabbah, IV, 4).

The child is born into a family for a purpose: to make of this world a better one than the world he or she entered. The male child is covenanted through the circumcision around the foreskin of the procreative organ, explicitly on the eighth day of his existence. In modern times, parallel covenantal ceremonies are celebrated for the female child as well.

The eighth day is legally and symbolically significant; so much so that should the eighth day fall on the Sabbath or on a festival, the circumcision covenant nevertheless must take place. On the eighth day, the infant has lived through seven days of creation. As such, the child is no alien figure thrown into a hostile world. The child is co-creator with God, coresponsible to repair the world. All things created in the first six days require further repair, since all things in the world are created incomplete. The circumcision covenant is itself taken by some sages to symbolize the need for the improvement of the self. There is something to be done with this unfinished world and incomplete self.

Other higher mammals are more completed in the fetal stage than are human beings. Humans, unfinished at birth, must create our universe, not out of nothing as in God's creation but out of the spirit given at birth. We are dependent on the environment and ourselves for repair and growth.

The child enters from a world of benediction into a world of benediction. The child comes with no maledictions attached to its nature. Not that it is expected that the child will not sin, for "there is no good human being upon earth who does good and does not sin" (Ecclesiastes 7:20). But should the child sin, it will not be because of some inherited flaw but because of natural human vulnerability. The transgressions are not traced to some original supernatural vice that can be expiated through supernatural intervention. Atonement can be accomplished only through the mind, heart, and deed of the self. No intermediary can be called on to do that work.

The child is born into a family that assigns him or her a name. Along with his or her own first name, the child is given the first names of his or her father and mother. The name is a dream, a hope, and a mark of continuity.

The child is born into the family circle that is enveloped by the circle of community. Whenever possible, a minyan of ten adults, the nucleus of community, is present at the covenantal induction. A quorum is required for all acts of sanctification. Communion with God requires the community of men and women. The boundaries of the self do not end with the body. The severed umbilical cord does not detach the child from its community. From birth, the child belongs. Not even the absence of circumcision nullifies the connection with the community. Not even an act of conversion into another faith obliterates the irreversible identity of a covenant. So powerful is the circle of identity that according to the legal tradition, a Jew however he or she may have transgressed remains a Jew.

Should the parent for whatever reason fail to have the child circumcised, the obligation to enter the child into the covenant belongs to the community. "Though my father and mother abandon me, the Lord will take me in" (Psalm 27:10). Should the infant be orphaned, it is again the community that embraces the child and offers this prayer: "Thou, God of all flesh, Father of orphans. Be thou a father unto him and he will be a son unto Thee. May his entering into the covenant be a comfort and solace to his mother and all his family."

Godliness is for the sake of life. However mandatory the rule that the child be circumcised on the eighth day even if that day coincides with the Day of Atonement, there is one marked exception. If the infant is ill, the circumcision must be delayed until he recovers. That ritual law reflects a tradition based on the sanctity of life. "You shall therefore keep My statutes and My ordinances which if a man do he shall live by them, I am the Lord." The rabbis repeatedly emphasized that the statutes and ordinances were given to be lived by, not to die by.

Bar/Bat Mitzvah

The "incestuous ties" of child and parent must be severed if the child is to grow into a mature adult. That severance is a process, sometimes a disquieting one. It is not surprising that there is some ambivalence felt by the celebrant and by the other members of the family at the ceremony. The bar/bat mitzvah celebration sanctifies the growing adolescent's spiritual identity. Both child and parents need to loosen their dependence in order to enter into newer relationships. Standing on the threshold of adulthood, the adolescent needs to let go of the security of total dependence. To be a bar/bat mitzvah is to become a responsible person subject to moral and legal imperatives. An ancient custom had the father pronounce a benediction after the bar mitzvah completed the benediction over the Torah: "Praised be he who has released me from the responsibility of this one." The child is morally accountable and henceforth is counted in the minyan that constitutes community.

According to a rabbinic insight, the *yetzer hatov*, or "good inclination," is developed in the thirteenth year of a child's existence (Abot D'rabbi Nathan 16:3). Before then, the libido prevailed. In the thirteenth year, conscience is born. With that birth the parents would be wise to let go voluntarily. The parents must step back to allow the adolescent to step forward. The bar/bat mitzvah at the synagogue service stands on his or her own to lead the congregation in prayer and the Torah without parental support. The study of Torah, the first of the blessings on the occasion of the child's birth—Torah, marital canopy, practices of good deeds—has been initiated. The induction of the child into maturity is exhibited through the mastery of the biblical text.

Parents understand that at this time of transition they must loosen their reins. It is not good to be alone, but it is not good to deny the adolescent the right of aloneness. Parents who live for and through their children inadvertently injure them. For their sake, parents should consider the counsel of the nineteenth-century philosopher Rabbi Samson Raphael Hirsch:

> If you rave of your children "they are mine" and where
> you should behold them as human and, in addition Jewish
> offspring, you see instead your daughter as a future house-
> wife or businesswoman or as an attractive beauty and wit
> or brilliant in her knowledge, as one who should be a
> source of support and joy and honor for you—or, espe-

cially in the case of your son, instead of educating him for
the one all-embracing purpose connoted in the designation
"human and Israelite," you seek only a mercenary divi-
dend in your efforts for him and bear in mind only the des-
ignations: businessman, craftsman, artist, scholar—and
you allow all the sublime that is connoted by the term
"human and Israelite" to be superseded by commercial
terms—then please do not speak of heavenly blessings of
children.

The rites of passage transmit the spiritual implications
of identity. In marriage the "I" recognizes its insufficiency
and discovers the inviolable "thou." In the covenantal circumcision there is disclosure of the "we" of the community; in bar/bat mitzvah or confirmation there is parental
awareness of the uniqueness of the adolescent self.

Who owns the child? In the *pidyon haben*, a rite that
takes place on the thirty-first day after the birth of the
firstborn son but that spiritually applies to all human
births, the child is released from priestly service to the
temple. Behind that ritual of redemption is the pervasive
religious insight that in the eyes of God human beings do
not own anything. They own neither land nor cattle nor
beasts nor spouse nor child nor self.

The child is not created to be formed in accordance with
parental ambitions. The child is created in God's image,
and therein lies the child's uniqueness and inviolability.
This principle underlies the rites of bar/bat mitzvah and
redemption of the firstborn. Parents are custodians of life.
There is no privately owned creation. "Sanctify unto Me
all the first born, whatsoever openeth the womb among
the children of Israel, both of man and beast; it is Mine."
People are borrowers, not owners, on this earth. No creation in the universe, animate or inanimate, other or self,

is an object to be treated any way one wills. Admonishing against human enslavement, God declares, "For they are My servants that I brought forth out of the land of Egypt; they shall not be sold as bondsmen" (Leviticus 25:42).

At the bar/bat mitzvah, parents of children on the threshold of adulthood may profit from the insights of the poet Nissim Ezekiel, a modern Jewish poet in India:

> Protect my children from my secret wish to make them
> over in my image and illusions. Let them move to the
> music that they love dissonant perhaps to me.

Death

If the rites of passage sanctify identity, define our spiritual reality, and locate our place in the circles of relationship, death threatens to destabilize and disorient the circle of the self. In which circle of relationship is the deceased self found? And where is the mourner's place? Graveside, the mourner stands between the living and the dead, between the world we know and the world from which no one has returned.

No one is more helpless than the deceased. The corpse is a metaphor for enslavement and passiveness. The psalmist whose soul is full of troubles feels himself "counted with them that go down to the pit." A man drained of all strength, he bewails his condition: "I am free among the dead, like the slain in the grave, whom Thou rememberest no more and are cut off from Thy hand" (Psalm 88:4–5).

The deceased is free of all commandments. Therefore,

the fringes of the prayer shawl that are placed over the shoulders of the corpse are cut or removed. The deceased is no longer subject to imperatives. He has no duties to perform, nothing for which he may be praised or blamed. "The dead praise not the Lord, neither any that go down into silence" (Psalm 115:17). All go down into silence.

Death reduces the image of the artist who formed the human being in his likeness. The Nobel Prize–winning Israeli novelist S. Y. Agnon suggested that the kaddish, the mourners' prayer sanctifying and magnifying God's name, is recited not to comfort the mourner but to console the Creator for whom the loss of every human being diminishes His own image.

The mourner dies a little in the death of his relative. While the dead lies before him, the mourner is exempt from the recitation of prayer, the donning of the phylacteries, the declaration of the Sh'ma, the pronouncement of God's oneness, and the love of God (Berachoth 3:1). Paralleling the tearing of the fringes on the prayer shawl of the deceased, the mourner tears his own clothing. Some commentaries suggest that the tearing of the cloth is a rite of resentment, an act of anger against the promise of life. The process of mourning involves separation and attachment, acceptance and transformation, a balanced relationship of Elohim and Adonai.

The casket remains closed throughout the funeral service out of respect to the memory of the person whose autonomy has been taken from him. In death, the person has become, in the rabbinic idiom, "as one who is seen but who cannot see." To expose the corpse and to allow those assembled to look at him comes perilously close to viewing the person as an "it." The casket is closed in honored memory of an active, willing, free personality.

There are limits imposed upon mourning. Excess in mourning is no act of piety. "Who mourns excessively for the deceased, mourns for another" (Moed Katan 27:2). Maimonides articulated the religious understanding of the way of the world. "One should not indulge in excessive grief over one's dead for it is said 'weep ye not for the dead neither bemoan him' " (Jeremiah 22:10). Maimonides interpreted Jeremiah to mean that the mourner is not to weep overmuch for the deceased. "For this is the way of the world and he who frets over the way of the world is foolish" (Laws of Mourning 13:11).

The mourner in his grief may wish to separate himself from the active community and to mourn in isolation. But the community will not abandon him. At the funeral, the community accompanies the mourners to the grave. The Hebrew term for funeral is *levaiah*, which means "accompaniment." It is the community that escorts the bereaved and the deceased to the threshold of the interment. At home it is the community that guides the bereaved back to the land of the living. According to custom, at the end of the seven days of mourning, the friends and neighbors of the mourner bid him rise from the low bench upon which he sits during the seven days and walk with him around the neighborhood so that the mourner may reenter the circle of the community. The community is at the side of the mourner before, during, and after the death.

Seven days of mourning are juxtaposed with the seven days of creation. In death a part of creation has been lost. It requires seven days to restore the memory of the lost and to rebuild the world of the mourner.

What of the deceased? Is he swallowed up into oblivion? What remains after the casket is lowered, the black ribbon torn, the earth covered over the grave? The deceased is kept in the circle of the living community through the art of memory. At the anniversary of death (*Yahrzeit*) and the commemoration of those who have died (*Yizkor*), prayers of remembrance are recited within the household of the community. Memory is an act of resurrection of the gestures, words, and deeds of the deceased. The deceased will not be forgotten. Memory sifts through the ashes of the past in search of the smoldering sparks of divinity.

The relationship with the deceased is expressed in the daily prayer as God's "keeping faith with those who sleep in the dust." The worshiper shares this promise of fidelity by remembering and acting. Immortality is dependent on the living. In remembering and in behaving, the living testify to the continued influence of the deceased and to the power of community.

G. K. Chesterton called tradition "the democracy of the dead" because it gives voice and votes to the most obscure of all classes, our ancestors. "All democrats," he wrote, "object to men being disqualified by the accident of birth; tradition objects to their being disqualified by the accident of death. Democracy tells us not to neglect a good man's opinion, even if he is our groom; tradition asks us not to neglect a good man's opinion, even if he is our father." Those who are remembered create memories that are bound up in the decisions of the living.

On the first day of his creation, Adam's world was a constant surprise. Everything was new to him, unexpected. At twilight Adam beheld the sinking of the sun on the horizon, the lengthening of the shadows on the earth, and the environment enveloped in darkness. He was convinced that the world was coming to an end. In terror, he flung himself onto the ground. His hands touched two stones. Upon one stone was marked the word *afelah,* "darkness"; on the other stone was marked *maveth,* "death." Adam rubbed the stones together and from the friction a spark of light was emitted. With it, he kindled a fire, made of it a torch, and was comforted throughout the night. In the morning, the sun rose and there was light. Adam had discovered the way of the world and the capacity of the human spirit to kindle a spark out of darkness and death.

The Afterlife

What happens beyond the circles of the living? Despite the rich rabbinic literature, the daily prayers that speak of "calling the dead to eternal life," and the *yizkor* prayers that refer to paradise, in practice the afterlife does not function as a major Jewish belief. Whether for an individual or a group, eulogies rarely if ever call upon the resurrection of the dead or the disposition of the soul in heaven as comfort or explanation. This despite the many contacts between Jews and Christians.

Jewish law is not obsessed with the transcendent world. Despite the praises of the everlasting tranquility and eternity of the hereafter, the religious man of Halachah (Law) prefers the real world, by which he means "this world." For it is only here that the human being "possesses powers to change anything at all."

Jewish this-worldliness may be a reaction to the passiveness engendered by other-worldliness and an excessive dependence on God's intervention. This is illustrated by the folk story of the pious disciple who boasted to his rabbi that he had saved the soul of a beggar who had come to him for a meal. The disciple offered him the meal but first required that he recite the *minchah* afternoon prayer, then wash his hands and recite the appropriate blessings, and then recite the *motzi* prayer over the bread. The rabbi chastised his disciple. "There are times, my son, when one must act as if there were no God in heaven or on earth." Hearing this the disciple protested, "Should I have acted as if there were no God, not have him pray nor wash nor recite benedictions?" The rabbi responded, "When a person is in dire need and comes to you for bread, act as if there were no God in the universe, as if there were no one on earth but you to help him." The disciple continued, "Have I then no responsibility for saving his soul?" The rabbi answered, "No. Take care of your soul and his body, not vice versa."

Not souls but lives are to be saved through the this-worldly efforts of human beings. "He who saves a single life is considered as if he has saved an entire world." Not only the refinement of the soul but also the sustenance of the body are the tasks in this theistic humanistic tradition."

The five books of the Bible make no explicit reference to the world to come, or to resurrection, or to heaven or hell. These beliefs entered much later into the Jewish tradition. Yet the yearnings of the soul for an afterlife find repeated expression in the Talmud and in later rabbinic traditions. There is a determination to hold on to both worlds. "Better is one hour of repentance and good works in this world than the whole life of the world to come; and better is one hour of bliss in the world to come than the whole life of this world" (Ethics of the Fathers 4:17).

The injustice of this world, the suffering of good people,

raises hope in the existence of another world. The world to come is a form of protest against a wretched status quo in which poverty, illness, and wars crush the human body and soul. Although the world to come may be exploited by those who seek to delay forever the tasks of lifting the fallen, it serves as a reminder that the world in which we live is incomplete, unfinished, unsatisfactory.

The afterlife may be understood vertically as existing in another place and another world. But the mourners' kaddish prayer itself does not refer to another place, another world, or another time, but to the mobilization of human energy toward the extension of divinity in human life.

An ancient Jewish legend speaks of the creation of Adneh Sadeh, literally a "man of the mountains," whose features were that of a human being—except that he was fastened to the ground by means of a navel string upon which his life depended. He could not wander beyond the tether of his life support. Should the cord snap, the man of the mountains would die. In this he was different from the Adam of Genesis, whose umbilical cord was severed at birth, freeing him to move, wander, change, and grow. This freedom marks his humanity. Freedom calls for separation and attachment. It is a process that runs like a thread through the rites of the enlargement of the self.

There is always some risk attached to entering a larger circle of relationship. The warmth and security of the more intimate circle is challenged by the extension of the self into a wider arena. One of the significant functions of rites of passage is to accompany the self from one orbit to the other. The minyan of ten Jewish persons functions as an extended family, the representative presence of community throughout all the stages of the self's growth.

Community is the constant referent in the prayers of the

rites of passage. In the crises of individual sickness or dying, the prayer unfailingly refers to the community. "May God have mercy upon you and send you a perfect healing among all the sick of Israel." "May God comfort you among all the mourners of Zion and Jerusalem."

When a death coincides with the festivals of the community, ritual law maintains that the family's mourning period be postponed. The joys of the community supersede the sorrows of the family. The grief of the family and the joys of community are not in conflict because the immortality of the deceased is tied to the eternity of the community. As the sages believed: "The community does not die."

The larger circle of community helps overcome the lure of familial selfishness, the closed family circle in which members live only through the family, oblivious to the concerns of those outside. Here charity not only begins but ends at home. Moral obligations are circumscribed by the boundaries of the family, and all who dwell without its borders are strangers. The circle of community helps break through the shell that restricts the network of relationships to bloodlines.

The concluding chapter deals with the border disputes between the circle of a particular community and the universal circle of humanity. It remains for many a major obstacle to Jewish identity and fidelity.

CHAPTER ELEVEN

Particularism and Universalism: Either a Jew or a Human Being

*Cosmopolitanism is likely
to be an alibi
for not doing one's duty
to one's own people.*

Mordecai M. Kaplan,
The Future of the American Jew

The tugs of conflicting loyalties may be triggered by a Jew bringing a Christmas tree into the home, or by the prospect of intermarriage, or by adherence to political ideologies. Who and whose am I? To whom do I owe my basic fidelities—to my own people or to the larger community of humankind? Is my identity that of a Jew or a human being? Sometimes it is asked starkly, "Why be Jewish?" Questions about the boundaries of Jewish identity are reflected in the tensions between particularism and universalism.

The Case For and Against Particularism

Particularists suspect the loyalty of those who stray from the communal family into the wider circuit of humanity. They cite the seductiveness of eighteenth- and nineteenth-century Emancipation and Enlightenment, whose promises of acceptance into the general community chipped away at the core of Jewish identity. The allure of humanism, internationalism, and universalism led to the erosion of Jewish identity. Toward cosmopolitan Jews, the particularists apply the biblical admonition: "They made me the keeper of the vineyards but my own vineyard have I not kept" (Song of Songs 1:6).

The penalty for assimilation is double alienation. Stranded between community and humanity, assimilationists can neither accept the rootedness of their particular community nor feel accepted by the world community. They constitute the body of marginal Jews who slip into anonymity or are absorbed by a negative community, Jews who associate only with Jews who don't associate with Jews.

The journalist Isaac Deutscher, himself a self-declared "non-Jewish Jew," could find no identity other than that thrust upon him by anti-Semitism. "If it is not race then what makes me a Jew? Religion? I am an atheist. Jewish nationalism? I am an internationalist. In neither sense am I therefore a Jew. I am, however, a Jew by force of my unconditional solidarity with the persecuted and exterminated. I am a Jew because I feel the Jewish tragedy as my own tragedy" (*The Non-Jewish Jew*). Ironically, Deutscher reflected that, "The greatest redefiner of Jewish identity has been Hitler."

The philosopher Sidney Hook confessed that he and many Jews like him were so enthralled by the promise of universalism that they came to regard concern with the suffering of their own people as mere parochial sentiment. "We were sensitive to the national aspirations of all other persecuted people, were positively empathetic with them. Yet when it came to our own kinsfolk, we lapsed into a proud universalism. We did not for a moment deny our Jewish origins but we disapproved of what we thought an excess of chauvinism" (*Out of Step*). Offering no such apology and more strident in her defiant universalism, Rosa Luxemburg, the international socialist of Jewish descent, turned on her fellow Jews in anger. "Why do you persist in pestering me with your peculiar 'judenschmerz'? I feel more deeply for the wretches on the rubber plantations of Puto Maya and the negroes in Africa whose bodies are footballs for Europe's colonial exploitation" (*Teller, Scapegoat of Revolution*).

Jewish particularists are upset by the pseudo-universalism that borders on Jewish self-hate. Surveying history, particularly after the Holocaust, they find the noblest vision of universalism naive and dangerous for Jewish survival and uniqueness. Some condemn the whole of Western civilization as a contaminating influence. For them, the proper antidote to assimilation is withdrawal into the protective circle of the particular community. The Talmud reports a classic debate bearing on the strategy for Jewish survival. When some of the rabbinic sages expressed their admiration of the engineering feats and aesthetic contributions of the Romans, Rabbi Shimon Bar Yochai responded cynically: "All these structures were made for themselves. The market places are to put harlots in them, the bridges to levy tolls for them, the bath houses to pamper their bodies."

Rabbi Shimon saw nothing praiseworthy in Roman civilization. He and his son Eleazar fled from that world into a cave where for twelve years they led a life of prayer and study. Once when they left the cave and came upon men plowing and sowing a field, they exclaimed bitterly, "People forsake life eternal for the business of temporal life." Aghast at the sight of what they took to be a misuse of time and energy, they looked with anger at society; and whatever they looked at was immediately consumed by fire. Whereupon a heavenly voice cried out, "Have you come to destroy my world? Get back to the cave" (Talmud Shabbat 33b).

Notwithstanding the divine rebuke of the cave mentality, a rising number of loyalists, especially after the Holocaust, insist that only the cave will shelter the people from the enticements of the world. Universalists counter that to be attached only to one's own community is to betray one's solidarity with the lot of humankind. Both sides err. They fail to differentiate between creative assimilation and slavish imitation, between loyalty to a particular group and the narrow insularity that suffocates.

Both should take to heart the perceptive passage from the rabbinic tradition that distinguished the subservient imitation of the Gentile world from the creative assimilation that enriches the particular community. The rabbis commented on an apparent biblical contradiction. In one section from the Book of Ezekiel, Israel is chastised for "not having followed the ordinances about you" (Ezekiel 5:7). Yet in another passage from the same book, Israel is rebuked for "having followed the ordinances of the nations about you" (Ezekiel 11:12). Rabbi Joshua Ben Levi resolved the problem. He explained that the latter passage refers to Israel's indiscriminate absorption of the corrupt features of the nations about it. The former passage rebukes Israel for its failure to select the elements of wisdom and beauty of civilization for the good of its own community (Talmud Sanhedrin 39b).

The transaction between the particular and the universal is analogous to eating food that comes from sources outside the self. Properly digested, the food strengthens the organism. To decline such external energy as alien is to starve. But to eat indiscriminately is equally dangerous. Substances inimical to the growth and health of the organism should be rejected. Similarly, to deprive Judaism of the experiences and insights of other traditions is to weaken Jewish vitality. Yet to incorporate an ideology that repudiates the reason for the existence of Judaism and the uniqueness of the Jewish people is suicidal. The transaction between the circles of relationship calls for a discriminating intelligence "to eat the date and throw the kernel away."

The restricted particularism that rejects the whole of Western civilization endangers the creative viability of Judaism. It is the dialogue between Judaism and other civilizations that historically has enriched the sophistication of Jewish civilization. The frequently cited abuse of science and technology in Auschwitz and in Hiroshima does not justify the wholesale rejection of their positive contributions. To reject science, the humanities, and the arts because they may be perverted to evil use is to curse the sun and moon because of idolaters who worship them.

Pseudo-Universalism

If particularism cannot see the forest for the trees, pseudo-universalism cannot see the trees for the forest. Cut off from its particularistic roots, universalism loses its natural ground. Universalism does not spring full blown from the head of its own visions. It arises out of concrete relationships within the family and the community. Aristotle understood that it is natural to love one's own family more than the families of others. It is naive to think that eliminating loyalty to one's own family will yield greater love for the families of the earth. On the contrary, the natural sympathy toward one's own family and people prepares the ground for cultivating generosity toward others. The philosopher Josiah Royce observed that when the spread of philanthropy and sympathy was "not founded upon a personal loyalty of the individual to his own family and to his personal duties," it became "notoriously a worthless abstraction."

To paraphrase the philosopher George Santayana, to love humanity in general is as foolhardy as the attempt "to speak in general without using any language in particular." The community is the particular language with which humankind may be addressed. Although the Bible originated from the needs and intuitions and revelations to a particular people, its wisdom and ethics burst into the public domain of humanity. The Holocaust is a uniquely Jewish tragedy but its lessons are for all of humanity. "When a Jew is beaten down," Kafka observed, "it is mankind that falls to the ground."

Martin Buber disagreed with those who urged him to liberate Hasidic teaching from its "confessional limitations" and to transcend it as "an unfettered teaching of mankind." Buber retorted that he was not bound to step into the street in order to speak to the world what he had heard. He remained in the door of his ancestral home; that did not shut it from the world.

The God to whom Israel prays is "the sovereign of the universe." Its voice is not directed to Jewish ears alone. It is out of the intense and close relationship with a particular people that Jewish universalism sounded its most resonant convictions. "I call heaven and earth to witness that whether it be man or woman, slave or handmaiden, the Holy Spirit rests on each according to his deeds" (Tanna de be Eliyahu). That which is ennobling in the particular community gravitates toward the world of the universal.

The governing biblical imperative "to love thy neighbor as thyself" (Leviticus 19:18) implies that the love for others requires a proper love of oneself. Altruism recognizes its connection with the values and concreteness of relationships in family, friends, and community. To pseudo-universalists who bypass the narrower circles to enter humanity at large, the response of Elie Wiesel to an interviewer is much to the point: "If you try to start everywhere all at once you get nowhere, but if you start with a single person, someone near to you, a friend or a neighbor, then you can come nearer to others."

Egoism and altruism form overlapping circles. This is illustrated by a folk story of the rabbi to whom a wealthy disciple came to boast of his abstemious ways. The disciple denied himself fine meats and expensive wines and was content to live on bread and water. To his surprise, and to the puzzlement of the other disciples, the rabbi chastised him: "My son, with all your wealth it is wrong for you to eat and drink bread and water. You must eat and drink with joy the finest that you can afford." The rabbi later explained his dissatisfaction with the stingy ways of the wealthy disciple: "If this man treats himself so shabbily, imagine how he will respond to the beggar who comes to him asking for food. He may think 'If I am content with bread and water, he should be content with eating rocks and sand.'"

It is noteworthy that the biblical tithing for the poor is to be given only after those who tithed rejoiced with "whatever thy soul desires, for oxen or for sheep or for wine or for strong drink" (Deuteronomy 14:26). Generosity rarely springs from the miserly soul, or the largesse of universalism from the isolated spirit.

The Songs of Self, Family, Community, and Humankind

As with the rites of passage, the festivals transmit the core values of the tradition through its legends and liturgy. They trace as well the circles of identity and their relationship to self, family, community, and humankind. The holidays reconcile the conflicting claims of particularism and universalism. Held together, the circles of self, family, community, and humanity meet in the unity of Godliness.

Without the larger circle of humanity, the circle of particular community succumbs to the conceit of chauvinism. Without grounding in a particular community, the ideals of universalism readily degenerate into imperialism. Without the circle of family, community, and humanity, the circle of the self collapses into provincial egoism. Without the circle of the self, the others tend to suffocate individual creative freedom. "If individualism understands only a part of man, collectivism understands man only as a part" (Buber, *Between Man and Man*).

The song of the poet and philosopher Rabbi Abraham Isaac Kook follows the expanding forms of spiritual identity.

> There is one who sings the songs of his own self, and in himself finds everything. Then there is the one who sings the song of his people and cleaves with a tender love to Israel. And there is one whose spirit is in all worlds, and with all of them does he join in his song. The song of the self, the song of one's people, the song of man, the song of the world—they all merge within him continually. And this song in its completeness and fullness, rises to become the song of holiness.

Oroth Ha-kodesh II, p. 458

The High Holy Days:
The Particularity of Jewish Universalism

Each festival celebrates both the unique and the universal embedded in the tradition. The High Holy Days are observed within the Jewish community. It is the season of

renewal for the observant and of return for those who
have strayed. The Kol Nidre evening of Yom Kippur is a
call to the alienated. The opening formula of the Kol Nidre
service extends an invitation to the distant: "By authority
of the heavenly tribunal and the court below, with divine
sanction and with the sanction of this holy congregation,
we declare it lawful to pray together with those who have
transgressed." The promise of forgiveness is offered to the
congregation of Israel as well as to "the stranger that
dwells among them."

The High Holy Days are for, by, and of the Jewish community. At the same time, the High Holy Days express
Jewish universalism. Rosh Hashanah does not commemorate the birth of the Jewish people, nor does it, as other
religious calendars, mark the birth of its founder. The Jewish New Year celebrates the creation of the universe and
the birth of Adam and Eve, the progenitors of humankind.

The liturgical language of Rosh Hashanah is particular-
universal. It addresses all of creation. "This day the world
was called into being; this day all the creatures of the universe stand in judgment before thee as children or as servants. Who is not brought to account on this day?" Within
the liturgy of Rosh Hashanah, the first covenant with
Noah, the progenitor of humankind after the deluge, is
recalled, praising God's remembrance of Noah "and every
living creature and all the cattle that were with him in the
ark."

The evidence of Jewish particularism and universalism is
apparent in the biblical selections read at Rosh Hashanah.
The Torah portion on the first day deals with Hagar, the
Egyptian wife of Abraham, and their son Ishmael. The
angel of God responds to Hagar's plea and protects her and
her son stranded in the wilderness. On the second day of

Rosh Hashanah, a parallel story of the intervention of the angel of God is told, this time on behalf of Isaac and Abraham. On the days that commemorate the birth of God's creation, the sages chose to remember both God's concern for Ishmael and Hagar and for Isaac and Abraham. Ishmael and Isaac are God's children. The particular-universal connection is exemplified in these twin readings.

The same spirit of particular universalism is evident in the rabbinic tradition that selected the Book of Jonah to be recited in the synagogue on the afternoon of Yom Kippur, the Day of Atonement. Jonah willfully turns away from delivering the message of Jewish universalism, determined not to preach to the non-Jews of Ninveh. What has a Jewish prophet to do with non-Jews? Jonah burrows himself in the cave of the whale's body, and for that narrowness of spirit, he is chastised. Though sent by God, Jonah's prophecy of doom against Ninveh is nullified because of the repentance of its citizens.

Jonah had not understood that God is the "God of heaven who made sea and dry land" (Genesis 1:9), who rules the sea, commands the wind, and reveals Himself in a foreign land. Jonah forgot that God's mercy is everywhere and over all His works. "And when God saw their works that they turned from their evil ways God repented of the evil which he said he would do unto them; and he did it not."

Jonah denied the redemptive character of Judaism. Within the tradition, Jonah is not deemed an ideal prophet because even though he thought to defend the honor of Israel, he offended the honor of God (Mechilta Bo). The ideal prophet is one who is concerned with both the honor of the Father (God) and of the son (Israel). Jonah misguidedly ignored the honor of the Father. He ignored Abraham's courageous contention with God on behalf of the non-Jews of Sodom and Gomorrah who were not of his kin, kith, or faith. Out of misplaced loyalty to his people, he forgot that he was a child of Abraham who was told by God, "In thee shall all the families of the earth be blessed" (Genesis 12:3).

The *shofar*, or "ram's horn," is sounded in the synagogue on Rosh Hashanah and at the end of the Yom Kippur service. Natan Sharansky, the Jewish refusnik, notes that the ram's horn is narrow at one end and wide at the other. Nothing happens when you blow through the wide end. But if you blow into the narrow end, the call of the shofar rings loud and true. The narrow opening of particularism extends to the wider arena of universalism.

The parable is particularly apt for Sharansky. Active on behalf of Jewish immigration, he struggled as well for the rights of Pentecostals, Catholics, Ukrainians, and Crimean Tatars. Sharansky came to realize in the prisons of the Soviet Union that there was no exclusive either/or choice between loyalty to his Jewish roots and to the ideals of universalism: "Only he who understands his own identity and has already become a free person can work effectively for the human rights of others." In retrospect, he observed that helping other persecuted people became part of his own freedom only after he had returned to his Jewish roots. Either Jew or human being is a perniciously false choice.

In the previous chapter I drew the self as central to the expanding relations that express Godliness. A society that values individualism is appprehensive lest the individual be overwhelmed by the community. Yom Kippur, more than any other day, speaks to the solitary individual and protects him from subordination to the group. No group events are associated with the fast of Yom Kippur. It commemorates no splitting of the sea, or wandering the desert seeking the shelter of the tabernacle, or receiving the revelation of God at Sinai, or celebrating a victory over the enemy. There are sparse external ritual symbols upon which to rely. On Yom Kippur, the individual cannot hide behind history or ritual or the skirts of community. Stripped bare of ceremonies, the individual wears a white kittel reminiscent of the shroud of death. The self confronts its own mortality and its own transgressions. No one can sin or atone or die for the self.

The litany of confessions of the self enumerated in the Yom Kippur liturgy do not deal only with the transgressions between God and the self or between community and the self. They are directed toward the relations between the individual and its own self. The transgressions listed in the Yom Kippur prayer book do not deal with ritual violations or even deeds subject to the judgments of the courts. The sins refer to self-injury and the abuse of the inner life, matters beyond the reach of the law.

The circles of self and community overlap. The distinctive claims of each must be honored but not isolated. Insulated, the excesses of community may crush individuality. Isolated, the extremes of individualism may cast the self into a prison of solitary confinement. Spiritual balance is needed. On Yom Kippur, the private confessions are followed by public confessions. The overt, public transgressions are balanced by those of private, inner thought. Contrary to the popular notion that Judaism is essentially a religion of deed, the litany of confessions recited on the Day of Judgment have to do with emotions, feelings, and attitudes in the domain of conscience.

The injuries confessed focus on the hardening of the

heart, anger, greed, causeless hatred, envy, bragging. Maimonides noted the correction of the lopsided emphasis on ritual and ethical public behavior: "Do not say one need only repent of sinful acts such as fornication, robbery, theft. Just as a person needs to repent of these sins involving acts, so persons need to repent of any evil dispositions that they may have. Hot temper, hatred, jealousy, greediness, quarreling, scoffing, eager pursuit of wealth or honors, greediness in eating and so on. They are graver than sinful acts for when one is addicted to any such disposition, it is difficult to give them up" (Laws of Repentance 7:3).

Passover: Family and Beyond

Passover celebrates the birth of the Jewish people. Observed in the home, one of its central aims is to induct the child into the extended family of the Jewish people. The family traces its spiritual identity to its slave origins, to the tribes whose family tree is enumerated in the opening chapter of Exodus. The Passover Haggadah is the family album of the Jewish community.

"On Passover," the author Israel Zangwill declared, "Jews eat history." Around the seder table everyone partakes of the symbols and substance of the family meal: the old and the young, the wise and the less wise. Both grandchild and grandparent taste the same bitterness of slavery, the saltwater of the tears of oppression, the dry, hard bread of affliction.

The narrative transmits the shiver of history to those who have forgotten or who never knew. History recalled gives rise to inquiry. The seder stimulates the child to ask the tradition four questions. The hierarchy of the "four sons" or "four children" in the Haggadah places those who cannot or will not ask at the bottom of the list. Children must be encouraged to ask not simply to gain information but because asking is an act of freedom. Slaves do not ask. Slaves lower their eyes, bite their lips, and remain mute. If there is no one around the seder table to ask the questions, neither children nor wife nor extended family, the tradition calls for the one who is alone at the table to ask questions of himself. The answers to the four questions are obliquely given in the Haggadah. Not the knowledge of the answer but the courage of the question is praiseworthy. No one is too learned or too pious to be exempt from the inquiry.

Passover begins at home, but it does not lock its doors to the world without. The opening sentence of the Haggadah calls for an open door for all people. "Let all who hunger come and eat. Let all who are in need come for the Passover." The first wording of the invitation, according to the commentary of Rabbi Jacob Emden, is directed to non-Jews, to those "who are hungry for bread." The second half is for Jews who need to ritually celebrate the Passover. Emden bases his interpretation on the talmudic obligation to feed both the poor of the Jews and of the Gentiles, to visit the sick of both, to bury the deceased of both, and to comfort the bereaved of both (Jerusalem Talmud, Tractate Demai 4:3).

Those directed to recall their suffering in Egypt are biblically mandated, "You shall not abhor an Egyptian because you were a stranger in his land" (Deuteronomy 23:7). Why not abhor those who have ruled over your people with such a fierce hand? The rabbinic commentator Rashi, among others, explains that the prohibition is due to the appreciation that it was Egypt that opened its land to the children of Israel when there was famine in the land of Canaan.

Evil must be remembered, but goodness should not be forgotten. A place in the Haggadah should be found for the exploits of Shifra and Puah, the two Egyptian mid-wives who defied Pharaoh's edict to drown the male children of Israel in the Nile. The daughter of Pharaoh who violated her father's decree to drown the infants and reached out to save Moses is deserving of recognition.

In the synagogue as well as in the home, the ethos of Jewish universalism is pronounced, especially during the last six days of Passover. A group of psalms praising God is normally recited on all the holidays, but on the last days of Passover some of the psalms are deleted. Who can sing of the idols who have mouths, ears, noses, hands, and feet but who cannot speak, hear, inhale, touch, or walk while their worshipers drown in the sea? (Psalm 115). Who on these days coincident with the drowning of the Egyptians can praise God for his deliverance from our pursuing enemies while they met with such a tragic end? (Psalm 116). There is joy in the Passover victory, but no gloating. When the angels in exultation praised God, the God of Israel and of the world silenced them: "My children drown in the sea and you sing songs of praise?" The joy of victory is diminished and wine from the cups is spilled because the means to victory involved the death of God's children.

The cup of Elijah stands untouched. A nineteenth-century Hasidic rabbi introduced a ritual in which the cup of Elijah is unfilled. Passed around the table, every participant contributes some wine from his cup into the empty vessel. When the cup is returned to the one who is conducting the seder, he proclaims: "Israel is not redeemed except through their own hands." Passover is not only to remember yesterday, but also to shape a better tomorrow.

Jewish universalism is rooted in native soil. It recalls the prophecy of Isaiah, who in God's name declared: "Blessed be Egypt my people and Assyria the work of my hands and Israel mine inheritance" (Isaiah 19:23–25). The God of Israel and the God of the universe are One.

Sukkoth: The Festival of Inclusion

If on Passover Jews eat history, on Sukkoth they dance theology. Four different agricultural species are clasped together and waved and shaken three times in all directions—east, south, west, north, up, and down. The species include a *lulav* (a palm branch, a myrtle, and a willow) along with an *ethrog* (citron). The verses from the Book of Psalms that accompany the ordering of this waving read: "Give thanks unto the Lord for He is good, for His kindness endures forever" and "We beseech thee O Lord save us."

Significantly, the waving of the four species is suspended at the mention of the name Lord. One does not point anywhere when the name of the Lord is mentioned. If God were "there," the other places of God would be excluded. God is not spatially located. God's universalism is enacted in the gestures of ritual choreography.

Each species represents a different character of the human spirit. The aroma of each refers to the fragrance of good deeds, the taste refers to the flavor of reason. The species are interpreted to typify different virtues. There are people who, like the ethrog, possess both taste and aroma; they are gifted with the power of knowledge and the practice of good deeds. There are people, who like the palm lulav, bear fruit but have no aroma; they are involved in the practice of goodness but not in learning. There are those, who like the myrtle, carry fragrance but bear no taste; they are ethically involved but neglectful of study. And there are yet others, who like the willow lack both taste and aroma; they are poor in learning and in practice. Nevertheless, the willow is essential, and in its absence the entire ritual act is unfulfilled. To exclude the unlearned and the socially inactive diminishes the wholeness of the people. Holding the four species is an inclusive ceremony of wholeness, the embracing of diverse talents within the entire community.

During the festival of Sukkoth, a total of seventy sacrifices were brought into the temple in Jerusalem. For whom were these sacrifices brought? For the seventy nations of the world whose well-being is God's concern and on the moral agenda of the Jewish people.

The melodies sung, the foods eaten, the stories told all cultivate the threads of nostalgia that bind. I recall and retell the stories of my grandfather, who on Sukkoth repeated the tale of Rabbi Pinchos of Koretz. A master of the Talmud, Rabbi Pinchos once prayed that no one would come to him with his or her troubles because the inquiries robbed him of time with his books. His prayer was granted and he now had ample time for study. Before the festival of Sukkoth arrived, Rabbi Pinchos sought help from his neighbors to build his Sukkah, but his answered prayers for solitude and study kept his neighbors away. He built the Sukkah without the joy of community. On the evening that custom urges the owners of the Sukkah to invite guests to share a festive meal, not one of the villagers felt welcome to come. The rabbi ate, drank, prayed, and studied alone. The rabbi appealed to the patriarchs and the religious heroes of Judaism to come and join him as "honorary guests," who according to the tradition visit the hosts throughout the seven days. But no one would come. As Abraham explained: "I do not enter the homes which are closed to my children." Rabbi Pinchos came to understand that more than books are needed to be part of a holy community. He therefore prayed that his early prayer should be annulled so that he may again be interrupted by people who come to him for counsel. His earlier prayer was nullified and Rabbi Pinchos rejoiced in his renewal.

In the same spirit, Martin Buber confessed that in his youth he preferred books to people. Books are pure, dependable, made of spirit and the word. Books offer manna, while people extend "the brown bread on whose crust I break my teeth." They are a mixture "made up of prattle and silence." In his later years, Buber came to realize that, "I knew nothing of books when I came forth from the womb of my mother and I shall die without books with another human being's hand in my own. I do indeed close my door at times and surrender myself to a book, but only because I can open the door again and see a human being looking at me" (*The Philosophy of Martin Buber*).

Stories transmitted to family and friends convey the ethos of the festival. In my home around Sukkoth, a story was told of Rabbi Mordecai of Neschiz to whom the citizens of his small village entrusted a sum of money, so that on the week before Sukkoth he might travel to the city and purchase on behalf of the congregation a fine citron (ethrog). In that way the festival ritual on Sukkoth could be properly performed by all the villagers. Rabbi Mordecai left for his mission and halfway there came across a wagoner crying because his horse had died. Now he had no

means of support. The rabbi gave him the bag of his villagers' money and turned toward home. When he
returned, the villagers asked to see the ethrog, and the
rabbi explained what had happened. "What are we to do
then on the festival of Sukkoth?" the villagers asked of
him. He replied, "Do not worry. While the whole world
recites a blessing over the citron, we will recite it over a
dead horse." There is theology in that tale. Ritual, however important, is not an end in itself. More than knowing
the law by heart is knowing the heart of the law.

Shevuoth: Self-Revelation

The festival of weeks called Shevuoth or Pentecost centers
on the revelation of the Decalogue. The disclosure of the
ten words at Mt. Sinai opens with an introductory statement unique in the Torah in that it does not indicate to
whom the divine words are addressed. It begins, "God
spoke all these words saying . . ." (Exodus 20:1). Were the
words directed to each individual self, or to the community of the children of Israel at large, or to the circle of
humanity, or to all of the above?

The ten words spoken, say some rabbinic commentators, were simultaneously translated into all the languages
of humankind. The school of Rabbi Ishmael interpreted
the verse from Jeremiah "like a hammer that breaketh the
rock in pieces" (23:29) to refer to the splitting of every single word that went forth from the Holy One into the languages of the seventy nations of the world. Another rabbinic legend emphasizes that the revelation took place not
within national borders but in the wilderness, in the public
domain for all peoples to hear.

The Jewish particular-universal orientation is strikingly evident in the assignment of the Book of Ruth as the biblical text to be read and studied on the festival of Shevuoth. Ruth is a born Moabitess, and of Moab it is written: "An Amonite or Moabite shall not enter into the congregation of the Lord; even to their tenth generation shall they not enter into the congregation of the Lord forever." Despite this proscription and its biblical reiteration in Nehemiah (13:1), it is Ruth who becomes the great-grandmother of David, matriarch from whom King David and King Solomon are descended and from whom the Messiah is destined to descend. As if to stress the universal message, the Book of Ruth ends with a genealogy that is traced to Peretz, the son of Judah and the pagan Tamar, a Canaanite woman, seeds of the Messiah's ancestry.

The rabbis note that the Decalogue is described in the Bible as words written on "both sides of the tablet." This phrase, they claim, refers to the letters that were cut through the stone so that it could be read from either side. It was read by Moses the lawgiver as well as by the people who received it. The commandments are not for the masses alone. They are also for the leaders who hold up the tablet.

The legend of the letters that were legible on both sides suggests the applicability of the Ten Commandments for both interpersonal relationships and for relationships with one's own self. The words of the Torah are multileveled: particular and universal, for the sake of relations with others and for relations between the outer and inner self. The intrapersonal emphasis was a characteristic mode of Hasidic interpretation. Thus, while "Thou shalt not murder" refers to the killing of another, on a deeper level it means that you are not to murder yourself. How does one murder oneself? There are ways we choose death, die a thousand deaths, eat at ourselves through the tortures of self-recrimination and guilt. The other side of homicide is suicide. We are given blessings and curses, life and death. "Choose life that thou mayest live" (Deuteronomy 30:19).

Similarly, the reverse side of bearing false witness against your neighbor is bearing false witness against yourself. It is forbidden to testify against oneself, to make oneself out to be wicked, to see only fault in oneself, and to deny the goodness in oneself. Likewise, it is wrong to be unfaithful to another and as wrong to betray one's own conscience. We are not to covet the talents and possessions of others. The reflexive side of the commandment refers to self-coveting, which is to envy what we already have but do not appreciate. As one Hasidic sage put it, "Better to desire what one has than to have what one desires." Rabbi Simchah of Bunam summed up the intertwined relationship of the commandments. It is written that "Thou shalt not wrong another." The other may be Jew or Gentile, the stranger in thy midst or the native born. The other may be the self whom you must not wrong.

The Sabbath

The Sabbath is the diastole of the heart. The Sabbath is a day of deeper breathing, the dilation of the soul designed to drink in the harmonies between the self and its environment. Its intent is to counterbalance the systolic action of the weekdays that contracts the heart and arteries to impel the blood outward. The Sabbath is not for transformation, acquisition, domination. It is a time to loosen the pulls and strains of ambition and to become aware of the gifts of inner tranquility. The muscles that throughout the week squeeze the earth are relaxed. The Sabbath is for the sake of re-creation. It is the time of noninterference. The petitionary prayers of the weekday are silenced. The Sabbath prayers are for appreciation; their goal is equipoise.

Each day, an imaginative rabbinic legend declares, was assigned its partner. Sunday–Monday, Tuesday–Wednesday, Thursday–Friday. The Sabbath was alone and appealed to God for companionship. The Sabbath He gave to the people of Israel, and in the course of history, to humankind. The Sabbath is the thanksgiving prayer affirming the life of the universe: Blessed art Thou, Lord our God, who has enabled us to live to this moment.

The Sabbath is universal and particular, rooted in the creation of the universe and in the exodus from Egypt. It is a holy day that belongs both to the Jewish people and to the world at large. The fourth commandment to keep the Sabbath was for everyone: husbands and wives, sons and daughters, masters and servants, native-born and strangers within thy gates, for humans and cattle (Exodus 20:8–11).

The Sabbath is a remembrance of the creation of the universe and of the first human being created on the last day before the Sabbath. Adam was created from the four corners of the earth, from white and black and yellow and red soil. All of humanity is shaped by God.

The festivals and fasts are to be taken whole. To enter the synagogue on Rosh Hashanah and leave it on Yom Kippur is to cut off a branch from the Tree of Life. To isolate one set of distinctive values from the organic wholeness of Judaism is to worship a part as if it were the whole. The narrative of the spiritual journey, marked by the sacred days of the calendar, interrupted by inattention, breaks off the conversation in midsentence.

The religious calendar holds together the contrasting moods and ideas that the holy days address. The introspective solemnity of the High Holy Days is balanced by the exuberant openness to nature on Sukkoth. If the fast of the Day of Atonement calls for the affliction of the soul and the deprivation of the senses, the festival of Sukkoth invites the participation of every physical sense. The joyous abandonment on Purim is counterbalanced by the mourning for the destroyed Temple on Tishah B'av. The Passover, expressive of freedom, leads into the Shavuoth revelation of law. The grieving over the decimation of one-third of world Jewry commemorated on Yom Ha-shoah is followed by the celebration of the resurrection of hope on Israel's Independence Day.

The individual who participates in the unfolding of the calendrical panorama mirrors in himself the yearning of a people for wholeness. Private and collective strivings coalesce. The mystic philosopher and chief rabbi of Israel, Abraham Isaac Kook, describes the circles of individual and collective enlargement that reach toward the divine light:

> Each individual must first find himself within himself;
> then he must also find himself in the world about himself;
> his society, his community, his nation. The community
> must first find itself within itself; then it must find itself in
> all of humanity. Humanity must first find itself within
> itself; then it must find itself in the world. The world must
> first find itself within itself; then it must find itself within
> the universe which surrounds it. The surrounding universe
> in its generality must first find itself within itself; then it
> must find itself in the highest category of universality. Uni-

versality must find itself within itself; then it must find itself in the fullness that fills, in the highest light, in the hub of life, in the Divine light. (*Oroth Ha-kodesh* II, p. 461)

Epilogue: A Word to David

We have seen how one of the major stumbling blocks to faith is carved out of the quarry of either/or thinking. Either/or is the way we have been taught to ask questions and offer answers.

Whether speaking of prayer, magic, revelation, evil, ritual, or ethics, the arguments are presented in the form of hard disjunctives excluding all other alternatives. Either God or man, either supernatural intervention or human invention, either literal truth or fantasy, either a voice from above or one projected from below.

Split thinking is impatient with the variety of complexions and complexities in the religious tradition. It holds to a monistic mindset that assumes one and only one religious truth, one and only one understanding of the will of God. It has no tolerance for pluralistic perspectives of the sacred text. It clings to the dogma of immaculate perception.

But the entire tradition from which we draw inspiration is far from monolithic. I have throughout called attention to those vital elements within the tradition that have been ignored or repressed but which should be known. To paraphrase Goethe, that which we have inherited from our forefathers we must earn again else we lose it.

Your doubts, David, are precious. Many of them may be traced within the tradition itself. Rabbi Moshe Leib of

Sassov was convinced that God creates nothing without purpose, including doubt. Skepticism was created to keep believers modest. Skepticism is frequently the source of new religious insight.

Honor the questions of your youth and do not forget them. They reveal the early promptings of your soul in search for what is real and what ought to be more real. Do not remain dependent on the answers you were or were not given in your youth. There are more and better things within tradition than you were taught. Do not dismiss your doubts as evidence of your lack of faith. There are doubts that challenge encrusted belief and cleanse it of its atrophied forms.

Honor all the tenses of time and particularly the present tense that is so often overlooked. The present tense is a vital part of the temporal flow that comprises the divine name of YHWH, Was-Is-Will Be. Your here and now enables you with others to refine the treasures of the past and to fashion a brighter future. There is a community of searching men and women like yourself who will find in the moral heroism, wisdom, and spirit of a people the courage to withstand the mindless materialism of mass culture and the excessive privatism of our age.

You have much to gain and much to contribute to your people and their quest for meaning. You are part of an old-new people and an old-new religious civilization. Your challenge is to be both heir and ancestor of an ongoing tradition of four millennia.

Index